It's All About Time
How Companies Innovate
and Why Some Do It Better

Cover photography by John Furey
Cover design by David Peters
Book design by Alden Bevington

MindTime Media
www.mindtime.com

Pioneer Imprints
P.O. Box 600
Ross, CA 94957
www.pioneerimprints.com

ISBN: 978-0-9818318-8-6

Library of Congress Cataloging-in-Publication Data available upon request.

"It's All About Time - How Companies Innovate and Why Some Do it Better." John Furey

MindTime is a registered trademark of MindTime Project LLC. MindTime Maps, MindTime Framework, Time Styles, the MindTime Triangle, Tempo, The Wheel of Collaboration and the Wheel of Thought are trademarks of The MindTime Project.

All inquiries and bulk orders for this book should be addressed to: contact@mindtime.com

Printed on minimum 30% post-consumer recycled paper.

Dedication

To you.
Do your best work.
Everybody has value to bring.

CONTENTS

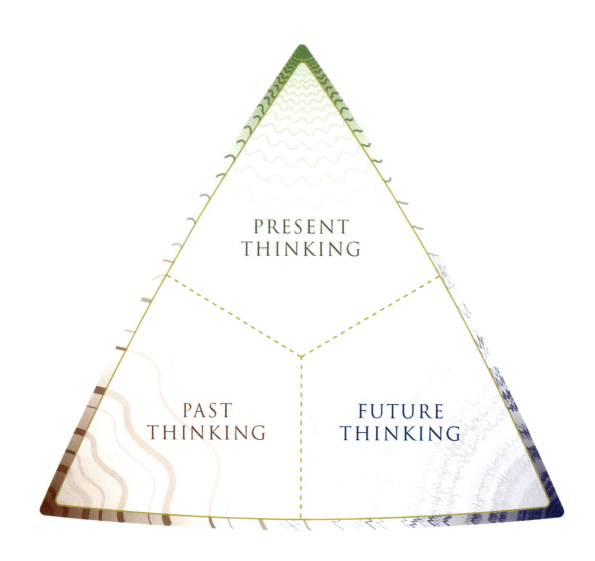

PRESENT
THINKING

PAST
THINKING

FUTURE
THINKING

THE MINDTIME® MAP

An Introduction to the MindTime Project

Right now, as you're reading these words, your thoughts are being shaped by three of the most powerful invisible forces known to humans. And, while I know you're quite familiar with their names, I'm prepared to bet that you're hardly even aware of their true power, which you could put to good use if you knew how.

These forces are shaping, influencing, and forming your thoughts in a most profound and predictable way, including your perceptions of what you're reading at this moment. Whether your first reaction is to be skeptical of what I've just said, wonder what these forces are, or be excited by the implications, you and your thoughts are being shaped by your mind's way of thinking—it's your survival system at work. Learning about these forces and their effects could very well change how you see yourself, your role in life, and everyone around you, for good, and for the better.

" It's your survival system at work."

The implications of this scientific discovery for business and the rest of our world are wide-ranging. Imagine being able to understand why people behave and think the way they do; to be able to predict their needs, motivations, preferences, and resistances; and to create a map of these influences at work in organizations and markets. But to develop this understanding we must first realize that humans live in two worlds: the world of physical being and the abstract world of our imaginations, our thinking minds.

We know much about the external, physical world; we have libraries of science explaining its laws and framing it within the three dimensions of space. The physical world is a world that has been at the center of our attention and study for several thousands of years. But what about the other world? The world we inhabit in our minds? The imaginary world of our thoughts? Discerning the nature of this other world reveals extraordinary insights, insights that Einstein alluded to when he bid us to raise the level of our thinking if we're going to solve the problems of our own making. Another Swiss thinker, Carl Jung, made it clear that it was this inner world above all else that was the source of all our future and past woes and success. The reason is simple: it's because the way we think defines the world we create.

This abstract world is where our egos reside; where we imagine ourselves and our circumstances as we were, as we are, and as we wish to be. This is the world of ideas and their reinforcing dialogue. This is the world of time. And as Einstein specified, you can only really separate space from time with a hyphen—space-time—because these dimensions are inextricably linked. Ignore one or the other at your own, or your organization's, peril.

In this book we explore what I mean when I say that our inner world of time is as significant as our outer world, you'll begin to realize just how significant this perspective truly is. Human behavior and motivation become easily explainable, and, armed with this information, you'll see how easy it is to make things work right. Whether you subscribe to what I am about to explain or not, this idea is poised to become one of the most fundamental ways of understanding people in psychology, and by extension, in marketing and the business world.

For the past seventeen years, an eclectic group of dedicated specialists from a variety of fields have been pursuing this science of thinking. They've come to a simple but startling conclusion: because we live in time just as surely as we live in space, understanding how any given individual perceives time—what we call their Time Style-- can greatly increase and enhance their effectiveness.

The insights contained in this book are some of the fruits of this endeavor. There are many more. Learning them is akin to finding an owner's manual for your mind--discovering a whole new world of functionality and efficiency for something you thought you knew very well.

This book is a short, simple introduction to the concept of MindTime, a brief but essential guide to the fundamental insights of the science and how to apply them in organizing people together

"The way we think defines the world we create.."

more effectively. It presents a radically new way to understand and think about an organization, one that will ring intuitively true to anyone who has managed and worked with people for any length of time. This book will facilitate collaboration by helping to build better relationships and a clearer understanding (and appreciation) of each individual's contribution.

When you consider that everything that we do begins with a thought, you begin to realize the implications of being able to map organizations, or markets, or classrooms, or political constituencies, as thinking systems. Our approach has revealed beautiful constellations of thinking minds with this data. The results we've seen have been truly amazing. We believe that when you see how much sense MindTime makes, and how much of a difference it can make in your organization, you may find yourself sharing our sense of excitement and possibility.

This excitement has driven our team for all of these years to seek a bigger understanding of what it means to think. At the MindTime Project we are quite literally attempting to map the world of thought within the framework of time. We have been trawling the peer-reviewed scientific research to discover the unique human qualities associated with the various regions of the MindTime map. We've discovered that scientific research from numerous fields has been pointing to the framework and significance of time in shaping of how we form our perceptions and thoughts. And because time is universal, the insights provided by MindTime are as true for individuals as they are for organizations, communities, societies, and ultimately, our species.

" Everything that we do begins with a thought."

In this book you will encounter two main ideas:

The first is MindTime, a framework for understanding peoples' thinking minds. Though it's been known for millennia that humans think by using time, exactly how we use time to think has never been properly explained until now. We explain this relationship and show you how to harness thinking in constructive and positive ways.

The second idea you will encounter here is totally new. It's the idea of graphically mapping people's thinking styles using the framework of time. This enables us to see how each person's unique way of thinking relates to the thinking of others. When seen from this perspective, organizations suddenly change shape; they are revealed as thinking systems, with their specific imbalances and biases. For the first time, you will see your organization as a thinking organism--and so much will start to make sense. Here you'll find a carefully explained and beautifully illustrated model that will help you become a more effective manager and leader of people--by virtue of understanding what is really going on "underneath the hood." You'll also discover how to work with the people around you in a way that will bring ease and enjoyment to your life. Along the way, you might also discover some profound truths about yourself as a person.

Though the subject is thinking and time, this book is ultimately about people. It is about how we work individually and how we create things together. It's also about how we can lead more effectively. It examines our role in collaboration and how collaboration must work, at least at one level, in order to have long-term success. It's also very much about innovation, the magic of a whole new thinking system at work.

A Timely Meme

We have discovered that the simple principles of MindTime are so intuitively clear to most people that they are viral and take root naturally in organizations, communities, and families. In the thirteen-plus years that we've been using this model for teaching audiences worldwide how people think, create, and generally lead their lives, we've never met a person who simply did not get it. Not one.

The reason . . . we can all tell the time, and by this we mean that everyone can tell the difference between past, present, and future, the three perspectives of MindTime. All humans (except for a few isolated cultures) mentally view the world through these lenses of past, present, and future. Time is what gives dimensionality to thought. Time gives rise to the three most fundamental thoughts we humans can conceive of: certainty, probability, and possibility. These three primary concepts influence every thought that we think, and they have a profound effect on how we see the world and engage with it.

Past thinking keeps a record of our previous successes and failures, investigates the past, and seeks, above all, to understand what is right and true.

Present thinking monitors trends as well as our current assets and resources, plans towards goals, and manages the movement forward to those goals.

" These three primary concepts influence every thought that we think, and they have a profound effect on how we see the world and engage with it."

Future thinking envisions new possibilities, explores these opportunities with enthusiasm and conviction, and is constantly driving change and adaptation.

These perspectives of thinking fuel our creativity and direct our basic thought processes.

Each person blends these three perspectives in different ways, relying on each perspective to differing degrees. Thus, based on our use of the three perspectives, we each have different Time Styles, or thinking styles (we use these two terms interchangeably).

A New Approach

A generation ago, most companies were hierarchical and rigidly structured. People assumed stereotyped roles defined by the daily tasks they performed. For many reasons, this has become an increasingly untenable model, and as a result organizations today are much more fluid. Workers move around far more frequently, both within and between organizations, and their work is defined more by how they think than by what they do. This trend has brought innovation and efficiencies to modern businesses, rendering useless the old ways of thinking about organizations.

" Applying MindTime is one of the most highly leverageable actions to help your company be more effective and productive."

Applying MindTime is one of the most highly leverageable actions to help your company be more effective and productive. This book will show you how to map your own and your employees' Time Styles and, using the MindTime Maps platform, better understand, lead, manage, organize, and think about your organization. By the time you've finished reading this book, you will know how to utilize what is the most potent and all encompassing of human energies—mental energy.

You will have a 360-degree view of any problem and you will significantly improve your decision-making process.

You'll begin to understand how to master the innovation cycle, analyzing your options more effectively and minimizing short- and long-term risks.

You'll learn how to communicate more effectively with your clients and customers by providing a new kind of consumer intelligence for marketing, and a road map for developing strong client relationships.

This model has already proven effective in a wide range of settings, and to date, our San Francisco-based consulting company, MindTime Inc., has worked with executives in nine countries, providing tools for navigating change and dealing with complex markets and economies.

MindTime's model for understanding people is simple, what scientists might even call elegant. It is not a personality index per se, although it provides a framework that informs us about people's personalities with great accuracy. Rather, MindTime is a means to see and understand the invisible forces of thinking that drive every individual, every team, and every organization.

This model provides a compass in the blizzard of human movement. It is a powerful scientific tool designed for our digital age. It's also a deeply human insight into who we are as people, one and all.

– John Furey

San Francisco, June 2010

1

THE SECRET POWER OF TIME

At any given moment, your mind is performing at least one of three basic cognitive functions:

- Accessing the past for workable solutions

- Monitoring your current resources, and

- Scanning the future for new opportunities

These are evidence of personal survival strategies at work.

All three time perspectives also shape the roles we play in our organizations and in society at large.

Past thinking is represented by our academics, storytellers, lawmakers, and scientists. These folks are responsible for our collective wisdom and for passing that body of knowledge on to the next generation.

Present thinking is embodied by our warriors, accountants, strategists, and community leaders. These people are skilled at managing situations day-to-day, building our society's infrastructure, enforcing rules, and bringing people to consensus.

Future thinking is championed by change agents, social visionaries, inventors, and entrepreneurs. Their role is to push us out of our comfort zones and open our minds to new realities.

These are evidence of personal survival strategies at work.

When it comes to thinking, it all starts here. Our mental survival strategies are all based on :

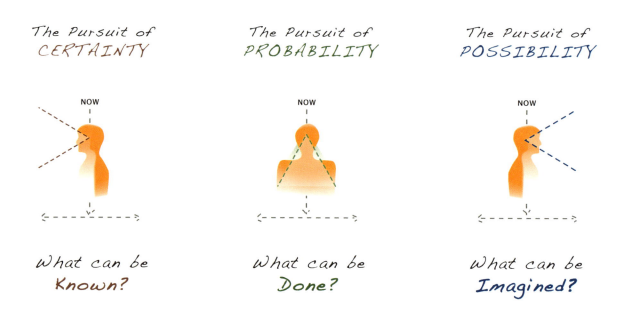

The Pursuit of
CERTAINTY

The Pursuit of
PROBABILITY

The Pursuit of
POSSIBILITY

What can be
Known?

What can be
Done?

What can be
Imagined?

The pursuits of possibility, certainty and probability are the most fundamental drivers of human thought: all our values, needs, motivations, communications, and everything else that is a product of our thinking minds can be traced to a blend of these three inter-dependent forces.

The most stable cultures—and the most stable companies—honor all three thinking perspectives and integrate their different strengths.

The trouble is, most of us tend to see the world through a single lens, our particular blend of past, present, and future thinking.

As a result, we perceive the world from a limited point of view and often come to view other perspectives as threatening. This mental bias limits our effectiveness and also causes a good deal of unnecessary conflict.

Over and over, we've heard executives complain that their management teams are easily derailed and fail to accomplish their primary goals. Upon closer examination, we find a growing tension between Past, Present, and Future thinkers, each of whom is fighting to dominate the conversation.

Generally, the leader of a group is unaware of these different thinking perspectives and has no framework and language to address the problem. As a result, the creative dialogue is derailed or progress comes to a halt.

Management teams make poor decisions not because they lack the right brainpower, but because their leaders don't know how to intervene and help Past, Present, and Future thinkers work in concert.

After you've read this book, you will no longer walk away from a meeting, wondering, "How could I have kept the conversation going?" or abandon a project, wondering, "What more could I have done to keep my team on track?"

With an understanding of the different Time Styles, you can take collaboration and decision-making to an unexpected, new level. You will no longer have to rely on mere intuition and fly by the seat of your pants. Instead, you'll have a scientific approach to team-building that tells you how to embrace different thinking perspectives and their different personalities and get them all to work in concert.

As you begin to understand yourself and others in terms of the ways you view past, present, and future, I guarantee that you will see immediate and positive results. What's more, your way of thinking about thinking itself will be changed forever.

As Einstein said, "You cannot solve a problem with the same level

You cannot solve a problem with the same level of thinking that created it.

We perceive the world from a limited point of view.

of thinking that created it." MindTime will help you to truly think "outside the box." In fact, it will give you a much bigger playground. As you begin to apply this knowledge, you will begin to transform your organization. So let's get started now.

How Do You See the World?

First, let's review the three basic thinking perspectives:

- Past thinking is the mental hard-drive that keeps a record of previous successes and failures

- Present thinking is the tool that monitors the work environment and keeps track of what's needed to do the task at hand

- Future thinking envisions new opportunities and possibilities

As noted, Past thinking dominates science, law, and academia. Research institutions are dedicated to building and adding to a cumulative body of knowledge.

The realm of Present thinking, with its overriding concern for maintaining order and managing outcomes, is most clearly seen in government. On a federal or local level, government is inherently conservative and therefore slow to change.

Future thinking is embodied in the corporate realm. Business and commerce are concerned with identifying new opportunities and with the seeding of new products and services. Entrepreneurship is a dynamic force that routinely embraces risk and change and is quick to identify emerging markets.

As a leader you must embrace all three thinking perspectives if you want your organization to succeed.

How Past, Present, and Future Shape Your Thinking

Most of us settle into a particular thinking mode. In any company you'll find people with very different values, goals, drives, dispositions,and

Our most stable organizations and communities have all three perspectives

Our mind's awareness of time generates these forces :

PAST THINKING	PRESENT THINKING	FUTURE THINKING

The Pursuit of
CERTAINTY

The Pursuit of
PROBABILITY

The Pursuit of
POSSIBILITY

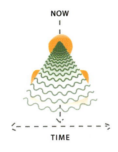

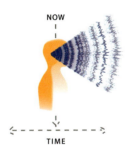

Past thinking patterns
generate awareness of
things
as they can be
proven.

Present thinking patterns
generate awareness
of things
as they are
currently
unfolding.

Future thinking patterns
generate awareness
of things
as they
could be.

17

anxieties. This is largely because of their reliance on one (or two) of the three time perspectives (some people integrate all three).

The variable distribution of these faculties among the population is actually beneficial to human survival.

Our most stable organizations and communities have all three perspectives. This allows them to maintain harmony, avoid past mistakes, and modify their values, when necessary.

History's most basic take-home lesson is this: To solve problems we face, we need to take full advantage of the insights of Past, Present, and Future thinking.

Thus the first step toward becoming a better leader is to become more conscious of your own Time Style.

Exercise:
Learn Who You Have Around You

Whether you ask your colleagues to participate in mapping their thinking or not, you will always be well served by knowing how the people around you think and what value they bring to the world.

Create a map for yourself of the people around you by making thoughtful observations about their needs, style, how they engage with their work, and how they make decisions. Don't judge these observations; that will only get in the way of the exercise. Don't assume you've "pegged" them, unless they've taken the Time Style Profile online at mindtimemaps.com. Be prepared to change your mind and revisit your earlier conclusions. Most of all, remain observant and empathic to others. Simply being open in this way will already change your experience of people greatly.

Now with your map in mind, step outside of the immediacy of situations and think clearly about what is going on, promote open conversations that call out the elephant in the room, and offer solutions. This book is full of them.

MindTime® illustrates how our minds bend time to create a framework that relates these forces equally to one another :

Our attention moves about within the framework of time much like our bodies move about within the three dimensions of space.

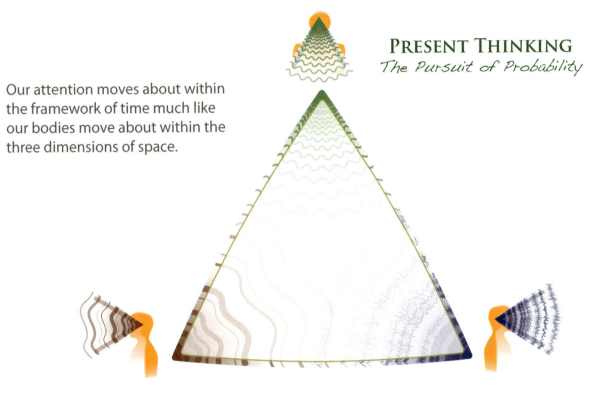

PRESENT THINKING
The Pursuit of Probability

PAST THINKING
The Pursuit of Certainty

FUTURE THINKING
The Pursuit of Possibility

Each region of the mind—Future, Past & Present—manifests unique skills, values and virtues, and each one is indispensible to our life :

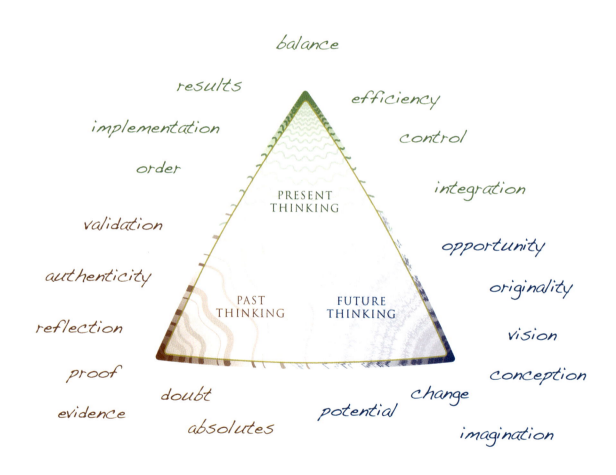

balance

results

efficiency

implementation

control

order

integration

PRESENT
THINKING

validation

opportunity

authenticity

originality

PAST
THINKING

FUTURE
THINKING

reflection

vision

proof

conception

doubt

change

evidence

potential

absolutes

imagination

2

THE THREE THINKING PERSPECTIVES

As you read the descriptions of the three basic thinking perspectives below, try to identify the one you use most often:

Past thinking gathers as much data as possible and is concerned with accuracy and truth. It refuses to take anything at face value; it needs to be certain and is perennially engaged in evaluating, validating, researching, weighing pros and cons, and judging credibility. Refusing to trust that "everything will work out," it attempts to reduce the risk of negative outcomes. Above all it is **reflective**.

Try to identify the one you use most often.

Present thinking seeks homeostasis and some measure of control over unfolding events. It monitors the surrounding world, assesses any changes in the environment, values stability, productivity, harmony, and closure and respects existing rules and the status quo. It will do everything it can to follow through and to honor commitments. It abhors chaos and confusion, and is driven to establish balance and order, create structure, and get things done. It is primarily **practical.**

Future thinking is open to possibilities, seeks out new opportunities and intuits what the future might bring. It is our source of vision, and it often promotes those visions with enthusiasm and energy, inventing new strategies and tactics along the way, and flying by the seat of its pants. It pushes the limits of what is known and understood. It is comfortable with change and ambiguity; it chafes when confined within a rigid structure. It needs deadlines for generating the motivation to bring something to completion. It is essentially **imaginative**.

Though all of us are moving into the future in clock time, these perspectives dictate how we think and what survival strategies we adopt.

That brings us to our next discovery: That each perspective has specific traits and limitations.

Past thinking gives rise to the skeptic who is always challenging new claims and trying to determined real danger from imagined threats. Its most common statement is "I'm not convinced you're right, and here's why." Past thinking can provide an important litmus test—or put up roadblocks, depending on the situation.

Present thinking is so keen on managing its environment and keeping a state of harmony in the moment that it may fail to see what lies ahead in the future. Its very need for order may keep it from properly navigating change.

Future thinking is always dealing in the abstract realm of what is yet-to-be. But it needs to take into account the wisdom of the past, and the stability of the present, before it leaps ahead. Its tendency to drive change for change's sake can be without reason.

Let's look at an example.

Amy and Mark are both managers at a firm that manufactures office computers. Lately, their meetings have been fraught, they've have been snapping at each other, and as a result, their product rollout isn't moving forward.

Amy, the lead marketer, is a strong Future thinker. Her role is to add new features, bundle new software, and increase the company's sales.

"If I have a new idea, I want to go for it," she explains. "I don't want to hear a lot of objections. I don't care if another company has tried something similar. I'm under competitive pressure and I just want to trust my gut and move ahead."

While Amy is trying to get through her presentation, Mark, the product manager, frequently interrupts, asking if other companies have tried the same approach. A strong past thinker, Mark wants to be sure the plan will work and so he keeps asking for research to back up her strategy. Amy feels that Mark is just shooting down her ideas, however, so she grows angry and resistant.

An organization's culture is usually the result of its predominant thinking style.

Amy, Mark & Collin are each approaching the situation from a different perspective.

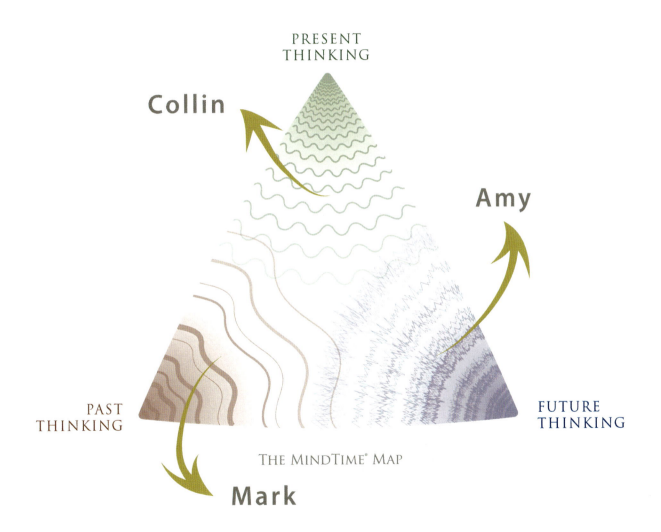

PRESENT
THINKING

Collin

Amy

PAST
THINKING

FUTURE
THINKING

THE MINDTIME® MAP

Mark

The president of the company asked MindTime to step in and help them find a solution. First we profiled and then explained Mark and Amy's thinking styles—then we described the important roles that each one plays in the innovation process.

"It's Amy's job to come up with new ideas," we said. "You can't fault her for that. She's just doing what she does best. She has to take the lead and be allowed to put all of her suggestions on the table. Mark's role, then, is helping her to find out which of these ideas is most likely to fly and appeal to your customers."

Mark realized that he had to give Amy free reign to come up with even the most outlandish ideas, because this was central to her thinking process. And Amy came to see that none of her ideas would get to market without Mark's careful scrutiny. What they needed was a better way to communicate, and a map that would help them use their thinking styles in the proper way.

When we mapped the thinking styles of the entire management team, we found a natural complement to Amy and Mark in Collin, the company's director of customer support.

A strong Present thinker, Collin is practical and process oriented. His management style is to move things forward by finding common ground and helping people reach consensus.

Present thinkers are usually good communicators who can talk to people "where they are," so Collin turned out to be the perfect addition to the discussion. He appreciated both Amy's need for innovation and Mark's reliance on past research, and he provided valuable guidance to both of his team members.

Now Amy comes to him to talk about a new product, before taking her presentation to the full management team. She knows Mark will want more information, so she and Collin start looking for some preliminary data.

When we mapped... we found a natural complement

"Once we start talking his language," Collin says, "it's a lot easier to get Mark on board."

The three colleagues are now able to joke about their different thinking styles and let each other have their say.

Mark sums it up, "Now we each know how to recognize our limitations and speak to one another's strengths."

Your Company Has a Time Style, Too

An organization's culture is usually the result of its predominant thinking style. For example: a pharmaceutical organization with a strong scientific and academic bent will likely have a Past-driven culture, while an advertising agency will constantly have its eyes on creative ideas and be full of Future thinkers.

In addition, a CEO with a strong dominant thinking style can set the tone for the entire organization.

Past thinkers are often chosen to carry on a legacy of engineering and design excellence. When Max du Pree followed in his father's footsteps as CEO of the Herman Miller furniture company, he continued the firm's tradition of hiring the nation's top architects and designers, and of offering employees a generous profit-sharing package.

When the economy hit a downward spiral, the company chose Michael Volkema, who appears to be a Present thinker, as his successor. Volkema had to make some tough changes to ensure the company's survival.

During his tenure, he closed the Georgia plant, downsized the staff, and sold an award-winning office building. He created a low-priced line of modular furniture and office lighting, then hired some Future thinkers to expand the business. Within five years, Herman Miller was no longer just a maker of office furniture.

When Hewlett Packard needed to update its image, it hired Carly Fiorina, an aggressive Future thinker. Fiorina was a high-profile CEO who turned HP into a major brand and spearheaded a merger with the computer giant Compaq.

Yet once the expansion phase was over, HP needed a very different kind of CEO. As the company's stock price began to dip, they let Fiorina go, and appointed Mark Hurd to make the company run more efficiently. Hurd was chosen for his strong Present thinking: his ability to track the nitty-gritty details of manufacturing and production.

Past thinkers value certainty and want to go with "the sure thing." Yet they can put their colleagues on the defensive with their constant need for proof.

Present thinkers are concerned with probability and managing on

You need people with different thinking skills.

The thinking style of more dominant voices within a company—
such as CEO—can have a more dominant impact on the overall
thinking culture of the organization.

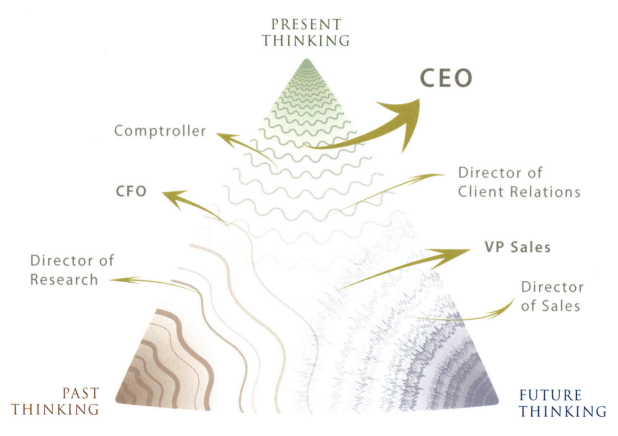

THE MINDTIME® MAP

Your Time Style also determines how rapidly new thoughts come into your mind.

a day-to-day basis. Yet they can resist being open to the future and change, or doing the kind of research that will validate their methods.

Future thinkers are geared toward possibility—their job is to identify new ideas and new opportunities and they too easily forget about the people who have to follow up on their many new plans.

Yet each of these perspectives contributes to the evolution of a business, and each needs to be called on at a different point in time.

By now, you're probably wondering what your Time Style is, and which perspective plays the dominant role in your organization.

The chart on the following page indicates the strengths and limitations of each thinking perspective—and the particular situations in which they excel. As you read it, see if you can recognize yourself.

Time Styles: The Key to Job Fit

You need people with different thinking skills, not just in top management, but at every level of your organization.

MindTime provides valuable tools for any executive who is putting together a task-force, committee, or creative team. And it's a boon to Human Resources as well.

The connection between job satisfaction and employee well-being has been clearly established. MindTime is providing a new level of insight into people and the roles they will succeed in most.

Future thinkers tend to find their natural spot in innovation and problem-solving roles. Past thinkers flourish in analytical, research-oriented jobs, and Present thinkers are superb planners and organizers, with an ability to make things run smoothly and keep everybody focused on the task at hand.

MindTime not only helps you identify the best candidates for a new position; it also helps you deal with "problem hires" and daily disagreements that end up costing money and slowing down your progress.

A brilliant engineer, John was promoted to head of the new products division. But whenever his colleagues came to him with new ideas, he'd find at least six good reasons why they wouldn't work. He was a strong Past thinker, and was the kind of person who always needed to be right.

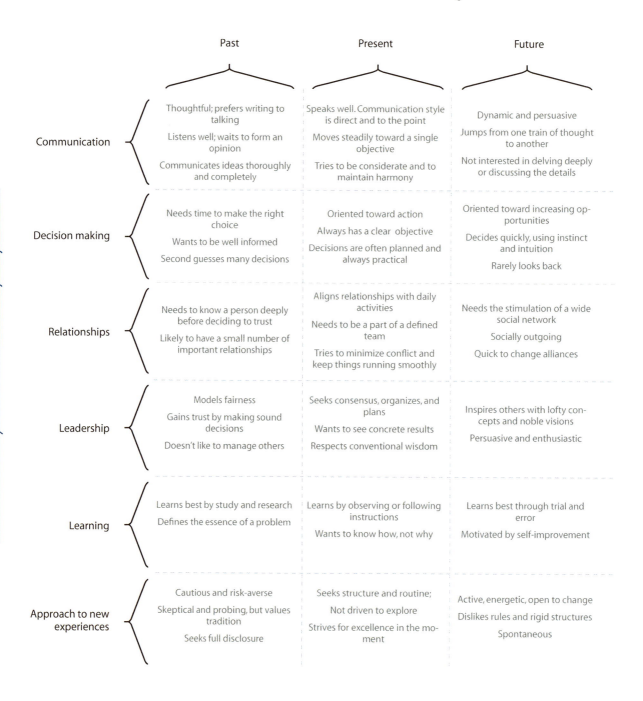

Situational styles for the three perspectives

	Past	Present	Future
Communication	Thoughtful; prefers writing to talking Listens well; waits to form an opinion Communicates ideas thoroughly and completely	Speaks well. Communication style is direct and to the point Moves steadily toward a single objective Tries to be considerate and to maintain harmony	Dynamic and persuasive Jumps from one train of thought to another Not interested in delving deeply or discussing the details
Decision making	Needs time to make the right choice Wants to be well informed Second guesses many decisions	Oriented toward action Always has a clear objective Decisions are often planned and always practical	Oriented toward increasing opportunities Decides quickly, using instinct and intuition Rarely looks back
Relationships	Needs to know a person deeply before deciding to trust Likely to have a small number of important relationships	Aligns relationships with daily activities Needs to be a part of a defined team Tries to minimize conflict and keep things running smoothly	Needs the stimulation of a wide social network Socially outgoing Quick to change alliances
Leadership	Models fairness Gains trust by making sound decisions Doesn't like to manage others	Seeks consensus, organizes, and plans Wants to see concrete results Respects conventional wisdom	Inspires others with lofty concepts and noble visions Persuasive and enthusiastic
Learning	Learns best by study and research Defines the essence of a problem	Learns by observing or following instructions Wants to know how, not why	Learns best through trial and error Motivated by self-improvement
Approach to new experiences	Cautious and risk-averse Skeptical and probing, but values tradition Seeks full disclosure	Seeks structure and routine; Not driven to explore Strives for excellence in the moment	Active, energetic, open to change Dislikes rules and rigid structures Spontaneous

Morale in his division was deteriorating; his staff no longer felt safe speaking up and had grown risk averse. The CEO trusted the engineer and didn't want to fire him. Furthermore, Human Resources didn't want to shell out the recruitment fees to replace a "bad hire." Since the department wasn't moving forward, the company called us and asked what they could do.

John was unable to interact with the Future thinkers that were key in product development, so we recommended he be moved to a role where his meticulous attention to detail and quality would be truly valued. As it happened, there had been issues with quality control in a number of divisions. John was well suited to this challenge. The CEO asked him to head up manufacturing quality control company-wide, and charged him with developing measures and standards for quality assurance. Today his team figures out how to improve the manufacturing process and make the production line run more efficiently. John's popular with his coworkers, and there's no more friction because his mission is consistent with his thinking style.

Warren Buffett, CEO of Berkshire Hathaway, once said he never fired anybody—he just found them a better job within the company. MindTime reveals why someone like John isn't working out. It allows you to evaluate every worker's Time Style, and tells you where each employee functions best.

I Can't Keep Up!

Have you ever felt like a meeting was hijacked by somebody who could spin out new scenarios at the speed of light?

Then consider this: Your Time Style also determines how rapidly new thoughts come into your mind and how deeply you are able to explore them.

- Past thinkers tend to be slower to respond and generally more reticent; they don't say very much, but all the while they're analyzing what's going on, investigating the depth of their experience, and when they do contribute something it is usually well-considered, penetrating, and relevant.

Warren Buffett once said he never fired anybody—he just found them a better job within the company.

29

Which characteristics seem more suited to quality control?
Which seem more suited to new products?
What does this suggest about the best use of John's talents?

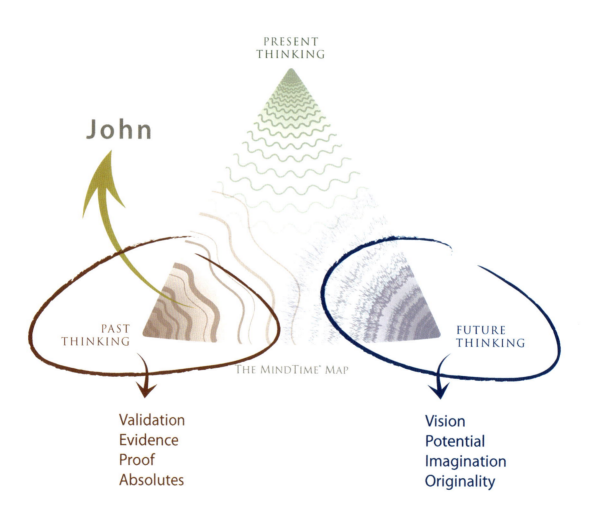

PRESENT
THINKING

John

PAST
THINKING

THE MINDTIME MAP

FUTURE
THINKING

Validation
Evidence
Proof
Absolutes

Vision
Potential
Imagination
Originality

- Present thinkers tend to plan their contribution to the conversation and wait for the right time on the agenda before engaging themselves. They make notes and rehearse what they are going to say and then proceed at an even pace.

- Future thinkers are full of new ideas and tend to jump from topic to topic in a highly creative and sometimes erratic vein. They are comfortable talking off the top of their heads. This is the quick tempo of Future thinking.

Of course, there are pitfalls associated with these different frequencies of thought.

A Past thinker takes the time to explore ideas in depth. This type is always searching for patterns and for the underlying meaning of events. Often the Past thinker comes off as being withdrawn, quiet, and painstakingly deliberate.

What's interesting are the blind spots of each thinking style.

A Present thinker is methodical, stable, and projects a sense of steadiness and calm. For Present thinkers, the mind's metronome tries to follow environmental cues with an even pace.

A Future thinker processes information quickly and then suddenly shifts their focus. Such people have a great deal of energy and enthusiasm. They talk a lot, and can be seen as mercurial and sometimes scattered.

What's interesting are the blind spots of each thinking style.

The Past thinker focuses on fewer thoughts, and can spend too much time reflecting on each of them thoroughly.

The Present thinker tracks with what is happening around them but can lack diversity of thought or depth.

The Future thinker entertains a large number of possibilities, but does not examine any one of them in depth.

What can you do with this information? If you notice people fidgeting because the pace of a meeting is too slow, you'll need to ask your Past thinker to move on and sum things up.

If a Present thinker is in control, the meeting will probably progress at an even, steady rate. Always based on an agenda, perhaps too rigidly?

But, if a Future thinker is in charge, you may have to ask for a recap, since that individual is likely to stimulate more thinking than the group can readily respond to in the allotted time.

These three types also have distinct ways of communicating.

If you can't tell whether you're dealing with a Past, Present, or Future thinker, just step back and listen for certain common words or phrases.

The following list will help you to identify the thinking and values that he or she represents.

It will also give you an instant "Time Style" diagnosis, helping you to understand where a colleague or coworker is coming from.

This list also comes in very handy if you're trying to speak the language of a prospective client.

These three types also have distinct ways of communicating.

.the three thinking perspectives.

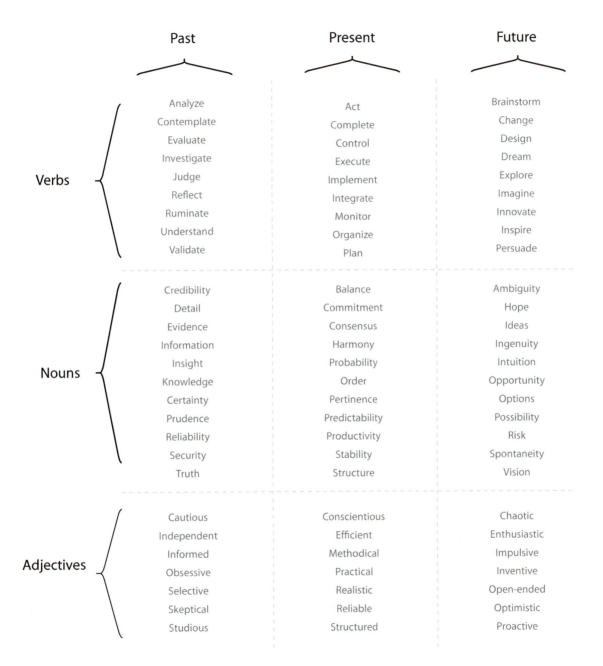

	Past	Present	Future
Verbs	Analyze Contemplate Evaluate Investigate Judge Reflect Ruminate Understand Validate	Act Complete Control Execute Implement Integrate Monitor Organize Plan	Brainstorm Change Design Dream Explore Imagine Innovate Inspire Persuade
Nouns	Credibility Detail Evidence Information Insight Knowledge Certainty Prudence Reliability Security Truth	Balance Commitment Consensus Harmony Probability Order Pertinence Predictability Productivity Stability Structure	Ambiguity Hope Ideas Ingenuity Intuition Opportunity Options Possibility Risk Spontaneity Vision
Adjectives	Cautious Independent Informed Obsessive Selective Skeptical Studious	Conscientious Efficient Methodical Practical Realistic Reliable Structured	Chaotic Enthusiastic Impulsive Inventive Open-ended Optimistic Proactive

Descriptors of the three perspectives

A Tool for Communicating

Brett, director of a Boston ad agency, had just pitched a print campaign to the CEO of a community hospital.

When he presented the storyboard, with the slogan, "Put your future in our hands," the CEO clearly wasn't pleased.

Brett did not resist the chance to learn more. "Just tell me what words you use to describe the hospital," Bret said, "when you take somebody on a tour of the institution."

"Well, I focus on what we're really good at," the CEO responded. "Most people know Mass General has a better cardiac unit and more money to spend on new devices, and the hospital is only an hour's drive away. So I tell folks about the compassionate care that we provide right here in the community. I mention that we're the oldest hospital in the state. Here physicians treat their patients just like family. We offer ongoing support groups and help people make lifestyle changes, after they're discharged. We're more than just an acute care facility. We're here for people day-by-day."

This CEO wasn't emphasizing the future—which is what surprised Brett the most. He didn't talk about advanced procedures and medical equipment. Instead he described Past values—the hospital's longstanding reputation—and Present values—ongoing efforts to help people monitor and control their health.

This is just one example of how you can serve your constituency better—by listening for their time perspective, you can identify the issues that are closest to their hearts.

Brett and the CEO see the value of a community hospital in different ways. Knowing this before developing his pitch might have generated a better client reaction the first time.

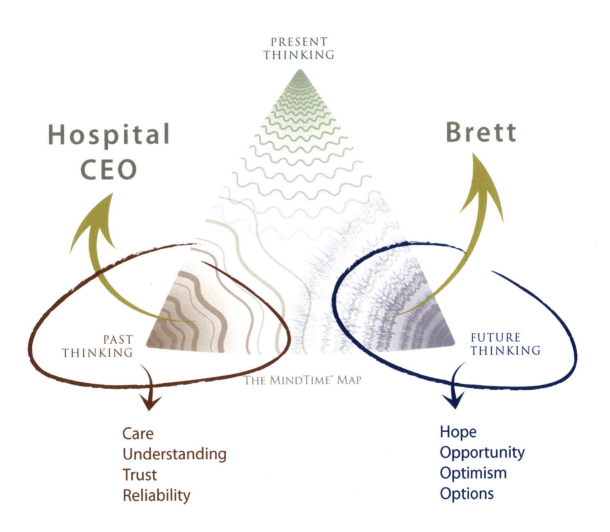

PRESENT
THINKING

Hospital
CEO

Brett

PAST
THINKING

FUTURE
THINKING

THE MINDTIME® MAP

Care
Understanding
Trust
Reliability

Hope
Opportunity
Optimism
Options

3

YOUR TIME STYLE

We've just explained three basic thinking perspectives—Past, Present, and Future.

Yet the truth is that most of us are hybrids. In daily life, we blend the three time perspectives placing a different emphasis on each.

It matters very much which perspective is in the lead.

Your Time Style may be Future–Past, Present–Future, or Past–Present, with your dominant perspective listed first.

If the dominant strength is reversed, you may be Past–Future, Future–Present, or Present–Past.

Finally, some people learn to draw fairly equally on all three modes of thinking. We refer to them as Integrated thinkers.

That gives us a total of ten Time Styles.

How do you find out what your Time Style is?

All you need is an Internet connection and about 4-5 minutes to respond to 18 basic statements. The TimeStyle Profile (www.mindtimemaps.com) will tabulate your results, and give you a result that looks like this:

It matters very much which perspective is in the lead.

The GPS for the Mind locates people precisely within the world of thinking. The closer a person's dot to a corner, the more dominant the influence of that thinking perspective in their life.

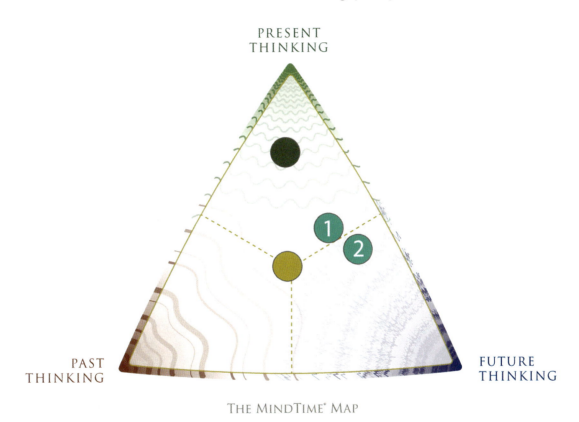

PRESENT
THINKING

PAST
THINKING

FUTURE
THINKING

THE MINDTIME® MAP

● The influence of Present thinking greatly outweighs Future or Past.

● Roughly equal blend of Future, Past & Present thinking qualities.

● Roughly equal blend of Future, & Present thinking . . . yet at '1' there is a greater influence of Present, while at '2' Future is more dominant.

The dot in the triangle indicates your relationship to the three time perspectives. If it's close to the center, that means you are fairly integrated in your thinking and are using all three perspectives equally.

The closer you are to one corner of the triangle, the more that perspective dominates your thinking.

If the dot lies equidistant between two corners, you blend those perspectives evenly.

If a coworker is on a completely different area of the map, you'll need to work hard to find a middle ground of communication. In the next chapter we'll give you some tips on how to engage them, and value what they have to offer.

What Does it Mean to Blend Two Thinking Perspectives?

Kate is the manager of a video production company and she easily combines Present and Future thinking.

She's practical and organized and keeps her daily planner up to date. Her colleagues think of her as a doer, someone who can be trusted to get things moving. She's also outgoing, energetic, creative, and full of new ideas.

In a given situation, she draws first on her Present skills, making sure that the flow of work is smooth and everyone is organized.

When she's satisfied, she moves on to her Future skills: she starts looking for new projects to tackle, and ways to make their product better, innovating with new computer graphics techniques and evaluating new editing software modules.

What she's not particularly good at is Past thinking—slowing down to consider anything in much depth. As a result, her decisions are often impulsive and, in hindsight, not particularly well informed. She fails to properly inform herself and reflect before she leaps.

Michael is a serious, hard-working CEO at a large insurance company. He lives a very structured life, planning nearly every activity in advance. He sticks to a familiar routine and is known to be a very deep thinker, someone who makes compelling arguments,

The dot in the triangle indicates your relationship to the three time perspectives.

and "really knows his stuff."

Michael uses both Present and Past Perspectives. Like Kate, he tends to focus first on organization. But when she turns toward the Future, he turns in the opposite direction, seeking out the wisdom of the Past. His closest confidante in the company is his Actuarial Director. They are both passionate about identifying "best practices" and measuring results.

However, Michael is resistant to the Future Perspective—valuing the realm of intuition and imagination—and would far rather stick to what he can measure and prove to his satisfaction.

What can we learn from Kate and Michael?

Your dominant perspective is the one you rely on most often and the area where you are most capable of thought leadership. Your secondary perspective is the one you use to support your strengths— it provides a set of complementary skills.

Your least favored thinking style generally remains in the shadows. You may resist engaging with it and therefore be unable to tackle certain tasks. You can make a concerted effort to develop this thinking style and draw it out, but it will never come easily and effortlessly.

Your Time Style Profile will tell you how you combine Past, Present, and Future perspectives of thought.

And it will give you an especially useful way of recognizing the strengths and limitations off your coworkers.

The chart on the following page gives you a list of the essential traits of the blended thinking styles.

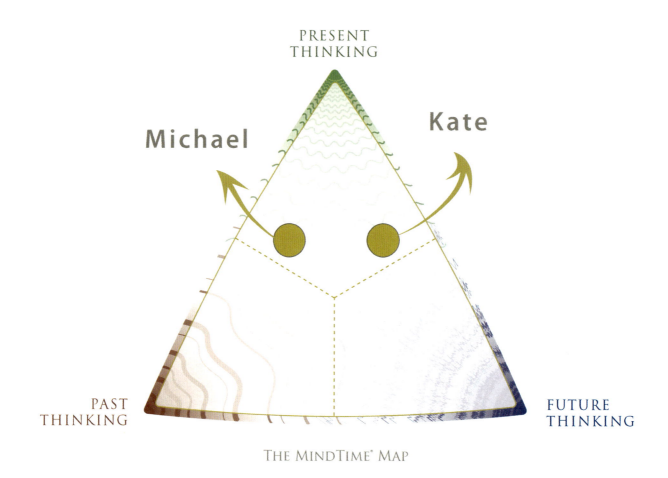

THE MINDTIME® MAP

Mapping Your Organization

Imagine having a map that reveals the invisible thinking forces at work within your entire organization.

The MindTime Maps web platform (www.mindtimemaps.com) allows you to do just that, and then shows you how Time Styles affect the way your business is working.

This came in handy for our client, Miriam, the VP of a new cosmetics firm in London.

When we met her, she complained that her corporate team didn't function very effectively. Several members were "talkers" who came up with all sorts of ideas, some good and some bad. In their eagerness to get things going, the team latched on to their ideas and tried to run with them, without testing out their feasibility. As a result, everyone in the company was working on too many projects with little regard to the possible outcomes.

In her spare time, Miriam also served on the board of directors of a local performing arts festival. This group was remarkably effective. The directors identified the groups they wished to support, found funding sources, and then worked hard to publicize the festivals.

Miriam wanted to know how to make her company more like her nonprofit.

We explained that each group was behaving in ways that reflect the thinking styles of their members.

Miriam's product-development team was dominated by Future and Present thinkers. It was innovative and focused on results, but lacked the critical, evaluative perspective of Past thinkers, who could help them to determine if ideas were trustworthy.

The arts organization, on the other hand, had a balance of Past, Present, and Future thinkers, allowing them to respond easily to the demands of adding performing artists to the festival, finding new backers, and growing their audience. Yet they also made sure the events run smoothly, and that they honored the patrons who had faithfully supported them in the past.

Miriam then wanted to know how she could use this knowledge to make her cosmetics company run as smoothly as her arts organization.

Each group was behaving in ways that reflect the thinking styles of their members.

41

We explained that most start-ups are formed haphazardly, often with little attention being paid to each person's contribution to the thinking whole. As the culture of a start-up tends to be one of uncertainty and chaos, Past thinkers almost never choose to work there and even Present thinkers tend to need Future thinking as their supporting perspective in order to survive the stress.

Miriam's company was not likely to attract the kind of Past thinkers that could help evaluate and measure the success of the various projects. Why? The risks for a Past thinker to join a start-up are just too great. By nature, they want to back a sure thing and are uncomfortable in high-risk situations. What she needed was a "Past thinker for hire," that is someone who would not have to rely on the company's income for survival, but who could give the group much needed feedback.

One of her colleagues at the arts organization had retired as the CFO of a public company and he fit the bill. His Past-Future thinking style provided the perfect balance. He loved the idea of entrepreneurship and yet had never had the opportunity to stretch his imaginative Future thinking. But, his Past dominant thinking style gave him the ability to ask the tough questions and demand provable results.

Imagine having a map that reveals the invisible thinking forces at work within your entire organization.

The team loved learning about this new perspective and welcomed the former CFO to their planning meetings. Very quickly they noticed a difference in their daily work. Instead of chaos and confusion, they felt a sense of purpose and began to take a steady, thoughtful approach to the planning process.

MindTime insight: *Before the actual work begins, the group should have a clear understanding of how they will interact, and what thinking style each person represents. Even drawing a simple MindTime Map on a piece of paper and placing dots representing the meeting attendees on it can have a profound affect on people's awareness of the group's limitations and how to navigate them successfully.*

That said, there are some departments in which a certain thinking style **appropriately** dominates. We spoke of the engineering team whose task it was to troubleshoot. This group needs Strong Past thinking—a careful analysis of facts and deep understanding of the fundamentals involved in the manufacturing process are essential to the group's success.

Present thinkers are likely to be hired in the loan processing office of a bank. Their task is to make sure the process goes smoothly for the applicant.

Past/Present Blend

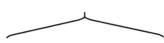

You love researching things in depth and thrive on details.

Knowledge and organization give you a sense of safety and control.

Your decisions are well informed and you're cautious, so you're unlikely to make mistakes.

You prioritize well, yet you can be flexible when the situation demands it.

You can make constructive changes to the status quo.

Past/Future Blend

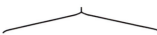

You want solid information.

You play it safe when faced with new and unexpected opportunities. Yet once you're sure of where you're going to land, you can take giant leaps.

You're both imaginative and grounded.

You may have trouble balancing your need for thoroughness with your need for variety.

Present/Past Blend

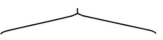

You excel at getting things done and doing things right.

To reduce risks, you follow trusted procedures.

You know how to take control and get things done.

You're conscientious, responsible, and thoughtful. You respect the status quo, understand its function and keep it intact.

The Six blends

Present/Future Blend

You're a planner, but you're also open to sudden inspiration. You have a strong sense of direction but are willing to take side trips or change course entirely when the right opportunity presents itself.

You have an appreciation for underlying patterns—you know why they're important in the bigger picture.

With your creative vision, you excel as a leader. With your eye for structure, you know how to nurture and build a strong organization.

Future/Past Blend

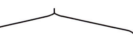

You identify opportunities, and then subject them to a mental vetting process, to be sure they will hold up and are worth pursuing.

You are a "quick study" and catch on fast to new ideas but you won't be misled by something just because it sounds great.

You consider many options in making decisions, but you know how to assess the risks. You're good at balancing intuition and hard facts.

Future/Present Blend

You always seize the moment—that's how you approach life in general.

You keep looking for better ideas and what's more, you know how to put them into practice.

You never let a good thing get away from you.

You are good at identifying opportunities and taking advantage of them.

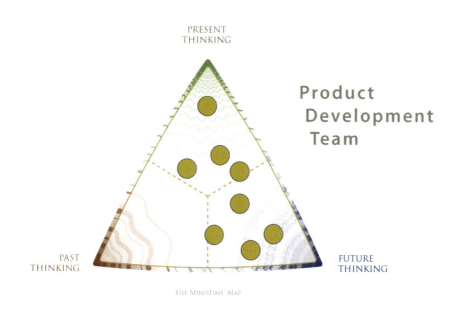

Product Development Team

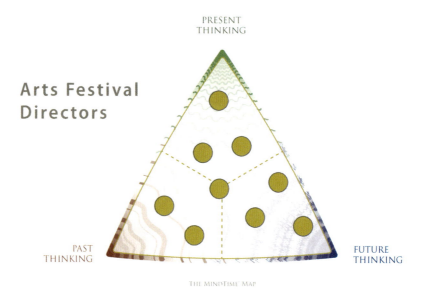

Arts Festival Directors

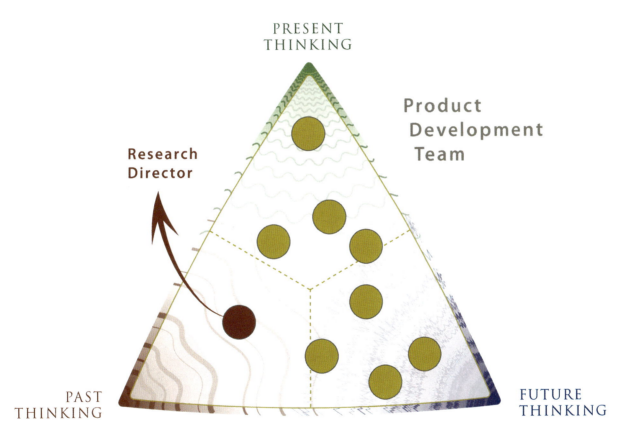

THE MINDTIME® MAP

A sales team needs strong Future-Present thinkers who can step up to the challenge and identify new opportunities while all along following through with delivering on the sales promise.

However, your management team must incorporate all of these Time Styles to be effective stewards and insure the company's vibrant continued growth.

Obstacles to Success

We've just seen how Miriam's company foundered due to an imbalance in thinking styles—and how this led to ongoing stress and conflict.

Minority thinkers—people whose thinking style is least represented—tend to feel undervalued and assailed. They withdraw, become defensive, or employ passive- aggressive tactics, thereby undermining the group's effectiveness. There are two ways to remedy this.

First, the group can recognize the critical importance of the under-represented thinking style and pay more attention to it. The dominant thinkers must not only give the others more airtime, they must regard them and treat them as vital to the group's creative process.

Second, the group can recruit more members with the minority thinking style until its makeup is more balanced.

Miriam rounded out her team with the retired CFO, asking him to participate in all management discussions. She explained to her colleagues that all new product ideas would go through a set evaluation process before they got the group's okay. Though she expected resistance from her Future thinkers, in fact, they were relieved. They no longer had to suffer the inevitable stream of failures.

The Present thinkers were happy, too, for now they would get to deal with details that were correct and only roll out products with a proven market.

By adding the missing link, Miriam was able to transform her entire organization and make every member of her staff feel more valued and effective.

When a thinking style is not represented at all, a company has a

By adding the missing link, Miriam was able to transform her entire organization and make every member of her staff feel more valued and effective.

serious problem. Its leaders are unable to recognize what it is they lack because they are completely blind to an important aspect of the thinking process.

The MindTime model indicates that companies like this are more conflict prone and their members are more likely to get stuck in circular disagreements. Tempers rise as people feel increasingly helpless. Without the missing perspective, they can't identify the problem and people become even more frustrated because they don't understand what's going wrong.

The following diagram shows the distribution of different thinking styles among the key people in two different companies.

Integrated thinkers, those who blend the three thinking perspectives almost equally, create lines of communication between people.

People who blend the three thinking perspectives equally, bring their own distinctive value to the organization. They may not be the people to lead research efforts or plan change strategies, or champion innovation, but they are the people who form the bridges and glue that bring together the other Time Styles.

Their ability to see each perspective, understand its value, hear its message and connect the dots is invaluable. While they are less likely to hold a determined point of view in the face of disagreement with a Stong Past, Present, or Future thinker, they will listen and be able to reinterpret what is being said so that others of different perspectives, who may be in disagreement, can hear it.

The key is to understand that their thought leadership style is somewhat different from that of the Strong persepctives or even Strong blends. Rather than being combative it tends towards being consensus building. This is often mistaken as being indicative of people who are less determined or less sure of themselves. In fact, it is the recognition that all points of view have value and need to be heard equally.

Integrated thinkers, those who blend the three thinking perspectives almost equally, create lines of communication between people.

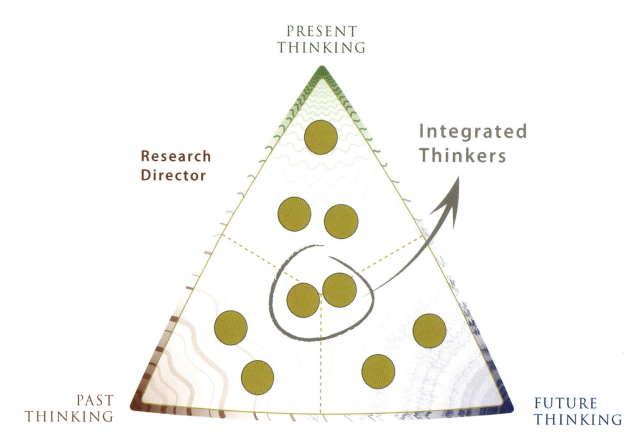

The MindTime® Map

4

THE KEY TO MORE EFFECTIVE THINKING

When you're feeling anxiety, stress, dread, or panic, it's often because you have to rely on a thinking perspective that you resist or underutilize.

We use the term "resistance" to describe those times when you feel at a loss, out of control, or simply out of your element. Your mind "just doesn't want to go there" because a situation seems too fraught or overwhelming.

The goal is not to let this resistance manifest in an unhealthy way. Some of our most notable inventors have had obvious resistances, and that didn't prevent them from succeeding. Albert Einstein came up with the Theory of Relatively but found it difficult to keep track of his daily affairs. Until the end of his life, he relied on his assistants to take care of his organizational responsibilities. Most likely, he was resistant to Present thinking.

The important thing to recognize is that every resistance limits your ability to function and in some way, impacts your self-esteem.

Your mind "just doesn't want to go there"

Your resistances can cause you to make poor decisions, disappoint others, fail to perform as expected, or make serious mistakes.

Therefore, it's important to understand them, and find ways to compensate.

Margaret is a strong Present thinker who is resistant to Future thinking. As the operations and products manager for a small mobile software company, she's been so focused on getting their core products to market that she hasn't had time to think about the kind of apps customers will want next.

Her solution to this was to dive in head first using her least used thinking style—her resistance. She would attend three major Expos, and bone up on the competition—and then go off with her three top software designers on an off-site retreat. "The sky's the limit," she told them. "I want you to pitch all of your best ideas. I want apps we can ride on for the next two years."

After the long weekend, Margaret selected a few ideas she found promising, and opened the door company-wide for new submissions. However, she quickly started to feel ungrounded and overwhelmed by the flood of new ideas she was entreating. She couldn't continue spending many hours a week listening to pitches for new products and reviewing employee submissions. She knew that her hard-wiring made her focus on creating order and certainty, and that her job was to see that the company delivered their software on time. But, she was able to change her focus just long enough to ensure their future and expand their product line.

Overcoming Resistance

Your resistances are not cast in concrete—you can consciously choose to develop other thinking skills. But it's important to set realistic expectations and not push yourself too far outside your comfort zone. I've often been asked how a person can compensate for a resistant perspective. The truth is that this isn't easy. No matter how hard you practice, using your less-preferred thinking perspective will always require much more effort. In fact, the following phrase sums it up: *When your nature gets in the way of* **your** *purpose, use self-discipline.*

The following chart lists the most common resistances of each thinking style.

Your resistances are not cast in concrete

Resistant to Past

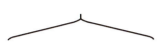

You may forget to look back at your mistakes and learn from them.

You may make decisions without regard for the facts.

You may be insufficiently critical of the information you use.

Resistant to Present

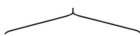

You may have trouble following through and getting things done.

You may find it difficult to manage details, stay organized, pay bills on time, be on time for appointments, meet deadlines.

You may have trouble honoring commitments.

Resistant to Future

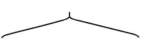

You may assume you've already thought of all the possible options.

You may forget to account for changing realities.

You may miss opportunities that could lead to greater success and happiness in the future.

Resistant to Past/Present

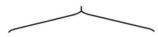

You may chase after every opportunity and end up feeling frazzled—without concrete results.

You may be overly optimistic about the chances of an endeavor succeeding.

You may get impatient and bored in certain situations.

You may make decisions too quickly, before you know all the necessary facts.

Resistant to Present/Future

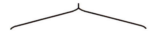

You may disregard the value of first-hand experience.

You may assume that everyone needs as much information as you to make decisions.

You may focus on risks without understanding all the benefits.

You may spend so much time gathering information that you fail to act or make decisions in a timely manner.

Resistant to Future/Past

Sticking to the rules may limit what you can achieve.

You may feel lost or anxious in situations where you're unable to follow a plan or working within a familiar structure.

You may be unnecessarily resistant to new ideas and experiences.

You may find it hard to trust your intuition.

Blind spots and resistances

51

Learning to use a less-preferred mode of thinking is similar to learning a new language as an adult. If you learn to speak Portuguese as a second language, for example, you will likely never be as fluent as you are in your native tongue. However, you can get to the point where you can communicate well enough to vacation or, if you really work at it, conduct business, for a time, in Lisbon or Rio de Janeiro. But, you'll find it especially mentally tiring.

If you're going to break out of your current mode of thinking, you need a strong motivation. Usually that comes with a "moment of truth" when you see how your thinking habits have put you in a box; it may be an elegantly constructed box, but at some point it will stop you from progressing any farther along your desired path.

Here's what you can learn from your neglected time perspective. This list is far from being exhaustive, but it includes some thumbnail wisdom.

If you're a Past thinker:

Here's how you can incorporate the insights of the Future:

- Make room for optimism and hope. This will recharge your idealism and help you find the degree of meaning that you seek.

- Take calculated risks—have the courage to seize the opportunity before it passes.

And here's how you can benefit from the Present:

- A sense of structure and the discipline of daily planning are your allies. They will make you more focused and efficient.

- Be open to order. Your deep understanding of things will have far greater value if you take the time to organize your contributions.

When your nature gets in the way of your purpose, use self-discipline.

If you're a Present thinker:

Here's what you can gain from the past perspective:

- Evaluate the status quo. If you find out what's wrong or less than optimal with the current system, you can start to make it better.

- Take the time to inform yourself. A plan is only as good as the facts and details it stands on.

And here's how you can learn from the Future:

- Seek out new experiences. Take the time to experience new people, new ideas, and be open to possibilities that might mean changing your patterns of behavior.

- Be spontaneous. Flexibility is good for your psyche. You also have a lot to gain by accommodating others.

Break out of your current mode of thinking

If you're a Future thinker:

Here's how you can incorporate the wisdom of the past:

- Start evaluating ideas before you act on them. Your decisions will be wiser and you will achieve better outcomes.

- Learn from your past mistakes. Commit to learning from them so you can avoid repeating them in new and different settings.

And here's what you can learn from the Present:

- Start less and finish more. Strive for more careful follow-through and you'll be more effective in bringing a new project to completion.

- Set specific goals and deadlines for yourself. Focus more on organization and you'll make more steady progress toward a goal.

Eliminating Barriers to Other Thinking Styles

Now that you see the possible benefits of being open to other perspectives, the next step is to focus on eliminating the barriers to change.

If you're like most people, your self-concept is tied up with your dominant thinking style. You're sure the world will stop if you no longer do what's expected of you and use the skills you generally rely on. But this isn't so.

Imagine for a moment that you are participating in a brainstorming session. Everyone is there for the explicit purpose of generating new ideas—a quintessentially Future activity.

If you're the Past thinker in the group you're going to have a very difficult time turning off the skeptic. But, if you insist on critically analyzing every wacky idea, you're only going to annoy the others and short-circuit the group's creative process.

For the common good, you must consciously let go of the part of you that wants to be critical and let pure unchecked creativity rule the moment. All that's needed is a **temporary** suspension of your Past thinking. If you are willing to refrain from questioning ideas and just wait, in time your underutilized Future orientation will emerge and you might even enjoy participating.

your self-concept is tied up with your dominant thinking style

The only way of opening new avenues of thought is to practice. You can't expect to learn a new language without actually using it regularly. You've got to force your brain to create new neural pathways and this can be unsettling. To exercise your less-preferred thinking perspective, just start asking yourself: Am I considering what the past/present/future has to teach me?

There is no evidence yet to suggest that a person can change their dominant thinking perspective. We are, after all, dealing with the human survival system and your mode of coping with the world is unlikely to change dramatically.

You can make this process a little easier, however, by leveraging your dominant perspective.

If you are a Past thinker, remind yourself you're about to gain understanding of yourself and the way the mind works.

If you are a Present thinker, set some immediate goals and work toward specified outcomes.

If you are Future thinker, think of expanding your thinking style as a new challenge.

Specific situations that force you to depend on a less-used thinking mode can be very useful in helping you change your thinking patterns.

You can go searching for these situations or just use the routine problems that come up every day.

Exercise:

Try to Change Yourself

It's not easy to change ourselves. Here's an exercise that can help lessen your resistance during times when self-change is desirable. It will help you understand what is going on between you and what is in front of you, be it an event, task, meeting, or relationship with another person.

Give yourself a gift: stand back from the situation for just five minutes. Ask yourself the following questions in the following order.

What am I being asked to do here and for how long? What thinking perspective do I need to call on in order to succeed? What's my Time Style? Where's the struggle? What's at stake?

By simply reflecting on these six questions you will do a number of things. You'll gain perspective on the situation. You'll acknowledge your strengths and weaknesses and get clear on what the real issue is. You'll put yourself in the place of making an informed decision as to whether you really want to commit to what is in front of you.

You will also release yourself from the unconscious mental struggle to change the circumstances you find yourself confronted with--a struggle that was bound to take hold if you simply ignored your feelings.

One word of note. Practice. No one ever succeeded in consistently achieving their goal without practice. Whether you want to really work at this to master your own use of the forces of thinking at work in your mind, or simply want to lessen your feeling of discomfort and struggle, practice this exercise often in little and big ways. You might surprise yourself with how useful it is to willingly change your own mind.

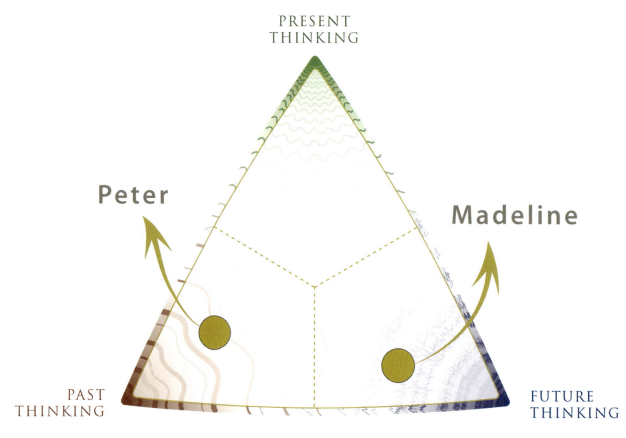

THE MINDTIME® MAP

If you're a Future thinker and your work area is becoming so cluttered that it's hindering your productivity, take a couple of hours to do nothing but organize. File things in files that are in front of you (you'll otherwise lose them for all time), consolidate, evaluate what's on your desk, and toss what's not important in the recycling bin.

If you're a Past Thinker, try spending time with a visionary, allow yourself to be swept up by that person's spontaneity, hang up your realism and practice seeing what is not there yet.

Are you a Present thinker, facing a big decision? Gather more information than you normally would before deciding. Or, dispense with specific plans entirely and go with the flow if planning is what you'd normally do.

For any particular task or activity, consider what would be your normal approach or pattern and change it. Turn it on its head and **change your mind.** This kind of conscious, radical situational pattern breaking can be transformative.

There is no evidence yet to suggest that a person can change their dominant thinking perspective

Another strategy is to ask for help from someone with a different time perspective. Peter, a Past Thinker, panicked when he heard his department at a major Internet consumer research company was about to be downsized. Then he went to his friend Madeline for advice. A Future thinker, Madeline immediately started looking at this as an opportunity. "You know this would be a good time for you to strike out on your own," she suggested. "You have the skills to set up your own analytics firm, and you know how often your dot com friends ask you for help in this area."

We all need friends like Madeline to help us see beyond our usual way of thinking. These people are happy to help because you've indicated that you value their unique perspective.

Once you've committed to overcoming your resistance, change may come more easily than you think.

To check your progress, you may want to take the Time Style Profile again. If you respond to the items with your new insights in mind, your results may change, reflecting this internal shift.

5

IMPROVING THE CYCLE OF INNOVATION

How many times have you seen a fabulous idea fail miserably, and sit there wondering, What went wrong?

It's generally because the people involved with that idea were thinking **in the wrong sequence.**

Until now, I've referred to the three perspectives of time in a chronological sequence, Past, Present, and Future. While this ordering of time perspectives seems to be perfectly intuitive, it also lies at the root of our failed thinking process.

To produce the best results with our thinking we have to do what only humans apparently, have learned how to do: bend time.

In our minds we can quite literally move the Past so that it sits between the Future and the Present in our thinking sequence. Future, Past, and Present. Why would we do this? Why would we mess with the usual order of time? To gain clarity and enhance creativity. This is the secret of MindTime.

After we've had a bright idea, we're best served if we stop and reflect on that idea and consider the consequences before setting it in motion.

Thus the new formula goes like this:

- Ideas—Future perspective;

To produce the best results with our thinking we have to do what only humans apparently, have learned how to do: bend time.

- Then reflection and consideration—Past perspective

- Then action—Present perspective.

Although, you'll find this wise insight being used in almost every serious endeavor—it is remarkably absent from our daily lives.

Most of us begin with Future thinking first (coming up with the idea), then move into Present thinking (putting a plan into action), and only later apply Past thinking, when we're trying to figure out what went wrong (and if you're resistant to Past thinking you probably don't even do that).

Yet this seemingly intuitive approach doesn't work. *In fact, you can usually count on it to yield a poor outcome!*

We've seen this happen over and over again. An inventor has a fabulous idea and then invests a fortune turning out a product only to find he is being sued for patent infringement. A company engages in offshore drilling and after a devastating accident finds out that its emergency disaster response plans are not at all well thought through or evaluated for a proper response.

In both situations, the train wreck might have been averted with the application of forethought, analysis, and research. The inventor could have done a thorough patent search before production. The oil company should have ensured, before it sunk its drill bit into the seabed, that it knew exactly what to do if it all went terribly wrong; then they would have been ready to act decisively in the face of catastrophe.

The MindTime approach involves re-ordering the thought process

The MindTime approach involves *re-ordering* the thought process. Here's how.

Your Optimal Thought Process

The optimal formula for innovation involves putting Future, Past, and Present thinking to work, in that order.

As your mind's *imaginative* faculty, the Future perspective helps you generate creative ideas. Since it is not bound to the past or the status quo, it often comes up with surprising and unexpected alternatives—and with outrageous opportunities.

Once Future thinking has done its work, these possibilities have to be sifted through, critically evaluated, and prioritized. This is the job of Past thinking. It helps you ask the right questions, weigh pros and cons, do the necessary research and define a level of acceptable risk.

It then falls to Present thinking to generate a plan of action.

Say you're in charge of a financial consulting firm and your clients seem to be dissatisfied with your current focus and products. First, you would want to engage your Future Perspective and ask what kind of investment opportunities do my clients get excited about? How can we use our expertise in a different investment strategy? You make a list. Then you use your Past mind to investigate the possibilities.

Your next round of questioning goes like this: Which companies have the financial products that I've envisioned in these new scenarios? What do I know about them and their reputations? What kind of training is needed for my brokers and support staff? Do we need to take on a new partner to lead us in the desired direction? Which of the strategies I've designed is both practical and desirable?

Once you settle on a choice, based on careful reflection of the consequences, you put your Present mind to work generating a plan: how you're going to finance the training or new additions to your staff, how soon you want to change the strategy, how you will move existing clients' assets to the new products without impacting their portfolios negatively.

The same process applies when you are engaged in launching a new career, a new product, or a new business enterprise.

Often you will have to go through several iterations of the Future–Past–Present process. When one phase is complete, you start over with Future brainstorming. Or, as you come across an unforeseen difficulty, you go through a mini-process of troubleshooting and re-evaluation, then continue along a slightly different path.

In other words, what we've painted as a linear process is really a cycle—or what we've conceptualized as The *Wheel of Thought*.

The Wheel is a wonderful image of how we move things forward and carry our vision to the desired ends.

The same process applies when you are engaged in launching a new career, a new product, or a new business enterprise.

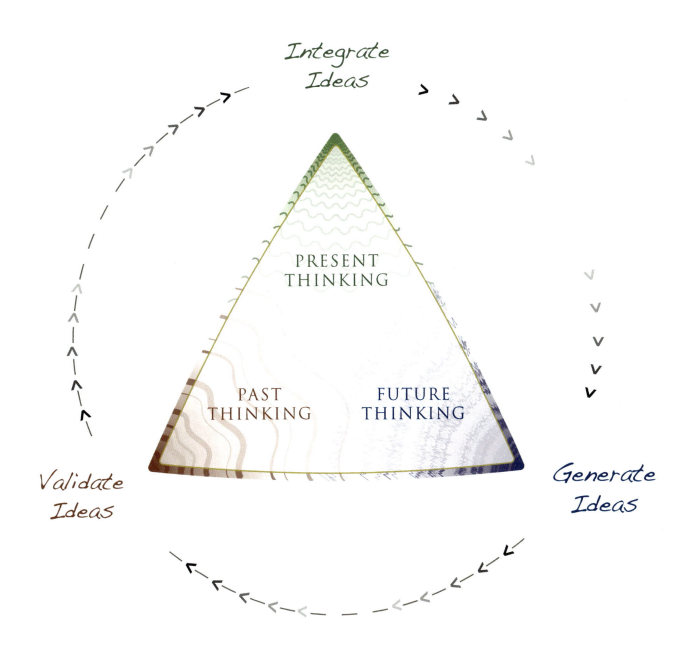

Integrate Ideas

PRESENT THINKING

PAST THINKING

FUTURE THINKING

Validate Ideas

Generate Ideas

The Wheel of Thought can be applied to almost any decision, problem, or project. Always begin with Future thinking.

The fragile seed of an idea (Future Thinking) can only start to take root once there is evidence (Past Thinking) of the idea's validity. This is like a process of natural selection. Once this idea proves itself viable and the consequences are understood, we find energy (Present Thinking) to bring it to fruition.

Rolling Your Resistances Out

Your wheel isn't going to move very smoothly if you're resistant to using any of the basic time perspectives. Indeed, it may not turn at all.

- A strong Future thinker may come up with fabulous ideas but never get around to analyzing them or putting them into action.

- A strong Past thinker may research and analyze forever without making a decision about how to move forward.

- A strong Present thinker will continue doing the same things and go nowhere because they don't break out of the status quo.

Without a doubt, you need to employ the awareness- building practices we described in the previous chapter to overcome your resistances and make your Wheel of Thought dynamic.

Yet the good news is this: the more you overcome your resistances, the more forward traction you're going to get.

Striving for perfection—and for total balance of the three perspectives—is not something I recommend. Instead, I tell my clients to get the Wheel in motion, in the right direction any way they can, then trust that it will gain momentum.

The Wheel of Thought will transform your thinking, slowly but almost magically. You will become more effective as you allow it to inform

The more you overcome your resistances, the more forward traction you're going to get.

the way you make decisions, solve problems, and organize projects.

You will still have limitations, but the Wheel will help you compensate for them. You'll stop making the same familiar mistakes and you may even experience a new burst of energy, like our client Jack.

You'll stop making the same familiar mistakes

Jack's boldness in seizing new opportunities was legendary. Well off, well liked, and well sued was how his friends jokingly referred to him. Yet while Jack had an intuitive flair for opportunities, he had less of a mind to spend any time investigating them before jumping in head first. On paper he was a success, but he found himself spending much of his time fighting inconvenient lawsuits—ones that he could easily have avoided if he had just done his due diligence. By midlife, this recurring pattern had worn him out and he was quickly losing his enthusiasm for the game.

The Wheel of Thought helped Jack understand his shortcomings, and it gave him a concrete explanation for his pain: He was avoiding the Past perspective altogether and spending all of his resources moving between idea and execution (Future and Present). Though he was celebrated for his quick wits and for pursuing opportunities, few people realized that this skill often landed him in hot water. Now, with more careful reflection, Jack was able to slow his pace and reap the benefits. He pursued fewer opportunities, and was careful to weed out those that were likely to backfire. And he loved being an entrepreneur again.

In the long run, you will become a more patient, tolerant, and well-rounded thinker

The Wheel of Thought tells you the order in which you need to engage thinking. And, if you are unable, due to a resistance in any of the three thinking perspectives, to bring the right thinking to bear, it tells you what kind of help you need to find, what kind of thinking to look for in others and to enlist.

It's easy to be self-critical—to see your failures as resulting from a basic flaw in your character. Ultimately, this is counterproductive and undermines your belief in yourself and your desire to succeed.

Yet failure comes from being tripped up by the very real limitations in your thinking. Some of the spokes in your Wheel of Thought may be a little rusty or even missing. But with a little practice, you can begin to restore and reinforce them.

In the long run, you will become a more patient, tolerant, and well-rounded thinker. And you'll bring that sense of balance to any enterprise that you direct.

6

A Model for Extraordinary Teamwork

The conductor flourishes her baton, and the string section offers up a poignant melody. The woodwinds, enter, and augment the sound—faint at first, but growing more insistent. The tempo speeds up as trombones, French horns, and timpani join in, and soon we are carried into the lush and passionate landscape of the symphony.

The members of the audience listen attentively, the music touches them deeply. Some listeners focus on the individual instruments— the bassoons underneath the oboes, the flutes fluttering above the violins—but what's really remarkable is the act of coordination required for this performance.

Ninety-eight musicians are playing *together* in perfect harmony and creating something of exquisite beauty,

Running an organization is like harnessing the power of an orchestra. To succeed, you need the proper score. And you need a way to coordinate the varied talents of all your coworkers.

Understanding the different thinking styles and their appropriate roles and value to the whole enables you to make a new kind of music. When leaders are working at this level, they have magic at their fingertips. And the entire organization begins to vibrate at a whole new frequency.

People begin to trust each other, communicate better, and appreciate the wisdom of their colleagues. And this allows them to move ahead with greater energy and enthusiasm.

Running an organization is like harnessing the power of an orchestra.

During a workshop, many years ago, I was asked if there was a simple way to read a person's thinking style, a set of visual clues that one could use to get even a rudimentary sense of a person's thinking style. I thought about this question for a bit and reflected on my own practice of looking for other people's value and likely contribution. And then it came to me.

I asked the workshop participants to use their index finger and wave it in the air as though it were a conductor's baton. First, I said, let's trace the mental energy of Future thinkers. Without too much thought, participants began to wave their fingers in the air in erratic and choppy motions, with sudden jerks forward. Next, I asked them to trace the frequency of Present thinkers. And again, with little hesitation, they traced their fingers in the air, this time describing an even wave.

The Wheel of Thought represents the most successful and reasonable way for us to think.

Finally, I asked them to trace the frequency of Past thinkers. This time, everyone drew a relatively flat line through the air. There was a burst of laughter, and seeing what had happened I explained that what might look like a flat line from up close, might appear to be a very deep wave motion when viewed from further away and over a longer time period.

So how do we get all these thinkers to move as a cohesive unit?

The Wheel of Thought represents the most successful and reasonable way for us to think. It's what happens when we have a good conductor in charge. And it also happens to produce the most sustainable results.

Yet it's not easy to achieve this kind of harmony in an organization. Why?

It is in general very difficult for a Past thinker to regard the Future thinker with anything but skepticism, at least until they're cashing large paychecks of an amount that the Past thinkers never imagined possible.

Simply put, the erratic and choppy mental energy of Future thinking has crashed into the long deep cycle of Past thinking. And from the Past thinker's point of view, Future thinking is just so much noise until it has proven itself valid. But they do prove themselves every now and again, and perhaps in more ways than we care to admit.

Without that risk-taking bravado of Future thinkers there would

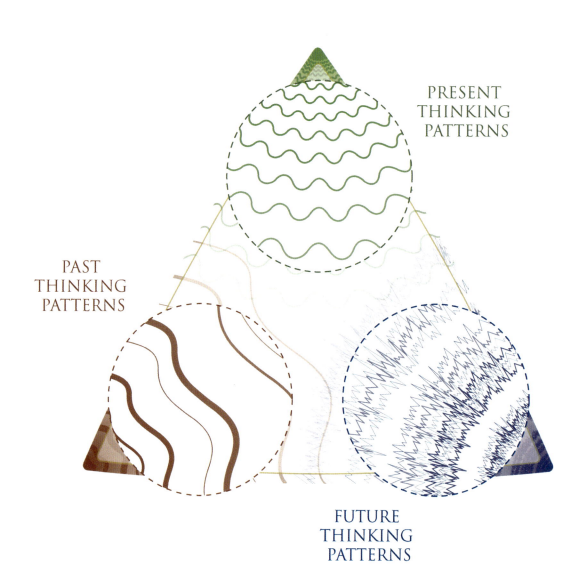

PRESENT
THINKING
PATTERNS

PAST
THINKING
PATTERNS

FUTURE
THINKING
PATTERNS

be no new ideas of any kind and no innovation. These courageous if somewhat ungrounded souls may sound like they're talking nonsense, but actually they're inventing tomorrow right out of thin air.

Past thinkers must develop a real understanding of what Future thinkers are doing and why Future thinking feels so uncomfortable to them. The key is building trust between these different folks. Past thinkers need to feel comfortable enough to listen and value what the Future thinkers have to say.

How can you make your particular way of thinking an asset?

Future thinkers, on the other hand, often label Past thinkers with epithets such as anal and rigid, stick-in-the-mud, and cynical. And from the Future's point of view, that's probably what it feels like when Past thinkers fail to appreciate what they cannot measure or predict.

The gap in these frequencies is like a great divide and only the most disciplined and mature groups actually manage to close it and collaborate successfully on a regular basis.

When you do achieve this balance, you will know it. At this point, every member of the team will be engaged in a deep and mutually respectful, collegial friendship.

It is essential for Future thinkers and Past thinkers to learn how to value what each mind brings to the table. When information flows smoothly between Future and Past thinkers, when each respects the other, the result is magical; present thinkers can now apply their knack for orchestration, picking up the flow, and all thinkers find themselves in a harmonious collaboration, rather than a deeply competitive conflict.

As a Strong Future thinker, I have had the benefit of working on MindTime with Dr. Vincent Fortunato, a Strong Past thinker. Our collaboration is born from the struggle to communicate across very different thinking styles, yet it has proved remarkably fruitful. Today we laugh on a regular basis about our very different time perspectives. Humor is a valuable aid on the path to consciousness. It helps us share our truths without the bite that sometimes accompanies them and allows us to temper our own responses to constructive criticism.

At the moment, the business world sorely needs more occasions where people work in concert. Much of what we do falls short of true collaboration, and the waste of resources and time is phenomenal. Most of us have the best of intentions, but this blending of people's

67

skills can only be achieved through conscious awareness and effort. It's all about people developing a newfound awareness and respect for each other's contributions, and making a concerted effort to appreciate the value of their thought process rather than judging the quality of each and every thought.

Your Role in a Group

How can you make your particular way of thinking an *asset* to the group and a contribution to the greater purpose? By being aware of your creative *role*. Your thinking style tells you where to look for your most important gift—and what you have to offer others.

Vision, truth, and productivity: these are the universal values that make a company effective.

For a management team to be successful, each value must be present and respected.

- If you are a Future thinker, you role is to carry the vision and ensure that your group embraces innovation, creativity, and receptivity to change.

- If you are Past thinker, you role is to gather true and accurate information and make sure the group considers it carefully.

- If you're a Present thinker, you role is to help things get moving, and your focus is on planning, flow, and harmony.

Let's see how this works in practice.

Bob, a Future thinker, is a partner at an accounting firm in Northern California. He wants to expand the business and knows that the only way that they can do so is to hire a rainmaker, a role he has traditionally played. The HR department has identified and interviewed many great accountants but no candidate has surfaced with both the drive and the contacts to bring in major clients.

When Bob reviewed the ads he realized that they wouldn't appeal to the kind of self-starter he was looking for. So he asked the HR department to highlight these Future values in the copy: a willingness

The gap in these frequencies is like a great divide and only the most disciplined and mature groups actually manage to close it and collaborate successfully on a regular basis.

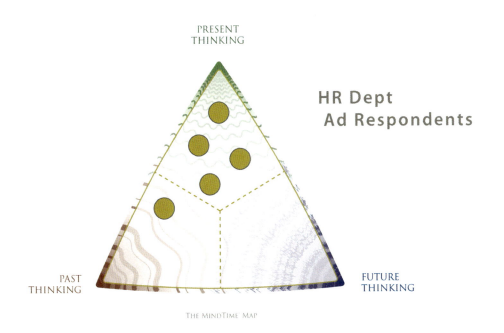

**HR Dept
Ad Respondents**

THE MINDTIME MAP

**Respondents to Bob's
Ad for Opportunity
& Expansion**

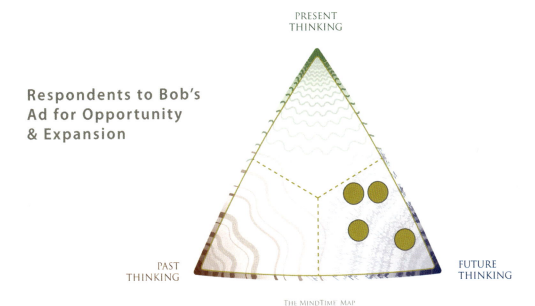

THE MINDTIME MAP

to explore new opportunities, identify new clients, and expand the business base. He also noted that the new hire had to be a self-starter, willing to work on a commission structure.

The next fifteen candidates were near-perfect matches. A few confessed that they were bored by numbers work and what they really wanted to do was to sell accounting! And of those, one of them had superb contacts. Bob stayed true to his values, and found the right person for the job.

How can you tell what person in your group is best-suited to what role, or, as with Bob, what you're looking for in a new hire?

The following chart describes the fundamental roles played by each thinking style. It will come in handy when you're in a position to serve as mediator.

With this information, you can provide the "rare link" between coworkers who are struggling to combine their different roles.

The Task of the Mediator

What to do when two of your best people represent opposing values and can't seem to get along? This is a question every leader has faced, at some point.

Jerry, a Past thinker, is the head scientist at a leading biotech company in Chicago. He's also in charge of quality control and he values the company's reputation. He's almost always at odds with Gene, the aggressive CEO who wants to rush the testing process and get the new device to market.

One day the chairman of this company came to us for help. We pointed out that the scientist and CEO were at opposite ends of the thinking spectrum and needed to respect each other's values. We coached the chairman and provided him with the tools and insights we believed appropriate.

The chairman sat down with both men and asked them each to describe their contributions to the company. Jerry cited research, integrity, safety, the lowering of risk, enhancing the company's reputation. Gene listed opportunity, making money, targeting new markets, seizing opportunities.

The chairman then began to mediate. "Do you think these values

They render the most important service of all, helping others find common ground.

Integrated

With your unusual ability to engage all Time Styles, you have a clear understanding of group process. You sense when members are focusing on only one Time Style and a minority perspective is being pushed to the margins. You serve as a mediator, help resolve conflicts, and keep everyone focused on constructive interaction.

Past

You help the group develop a deeper understanding of its mission.

You teach people how to reduce the risk of failure and measure progress realistically.

Your skepticism and independence militate against "group-think" and blind conformity.

Present

You keep your teammates focused on outcomes.

You ensure that goals are realistic and the group doesn't take on more work than it can handle.

You hold people accountable and make sure they honor their deadlines and commitments.

Future

You champion innovation, focus on solutions, and help others begin to think outside-the-box.

You inspire others and remind them of the bigger picture.

You help the group adapt to new circumstances.

Past/Present Blend

Information and organization are both important to you.

You're likely to manage the group's data, adding to it with your own thorough research.

Your caution and practicality provide a solid foundation for decision making. You help the group avoid unnecessary risks.

Present/Future Blend

Your attention to trends and changing markets is a valuable contribution to the group.

You encourage others to act in a timely manner.

You combine vision, action, and a knack for organizing. People say that you're a natural leader.

Future/Past Blend

You help the group set goals with a "grain of salt," insisting that their vision be backed up with solid facts.

You counsel against snap decisions.

You find it easy to motivate others because you're confident that your goals are viable.

Past/Future Blend

You ensure that the group makes decisions with full knowledge of the risks and consequences.

Others come to rely on your experience and wisdom.

You are good at detecting when rules and structures become too confining for the group..

Present/Past Blend

You create efficient systems--organizing information, people, and the flow of work.

A team player, you help the group stay focused on its collective goals.

You promote accountability, reliability, and trustworthiness, and help bring projects to completion.

Future/Present Blend

You make sure the group grabs new opportunities before it's too late.

You're more open to change than most Present thinkers, and understand the benefits of deviating from a plan.

You're an inspiring but pragmatic leader.

Contributions of the ten MindTime Archetypes

71

cancel each other out? If so, we haven't got a company."

Then he continued, "Is there a way we can formalize these values, combine them and build a stronger, better company?"

Jerry said, "I understand that in order for me to have a job, we need to get these devices to market. And that's Gene's focus as a CEO. My job is to make sure we do this in a way that contributes to our reputation for quality and safety."

The chairman turned to Gene and said, "To grow the company we have to deliver a successful product. How much time can you realistically give Jerry to complete the necessary tests?"

Working together, the management team came up with a timeframe to validate their product and bring it to market.

Often the people who make the best mediators are Integrated thinkers, people who blend all three thinking perspectives.

They may not be CEOs, but they are, in a sense, the emotional leaders or the company confidantes. These individuals are receptive and sympathetic, always willing to listen to a coworker's point of view. They don't step into the limelight, however, until there is a conflict or an evident need to bridge the gap. Then they render the most important service of all, helping others find common ground.

Often the people who make the best mediators are Integrated thinkers

Exercise:
Intelligent Meetings

Like moths to flame, we rush towards our goals without considering who we are and what is driving us.

If you are going to invest an hour with a group of people in a meeting and during this meeting achieve some kind of goal, you owe it to yourself and the rest of the group to take a few minutes to figure out what thinking styles are at work in the meeting.

Do you have the correct mix of people to achieve your goals? Are you missing a vital thinking style? Is one of the thinking styles under-represented and, worst still, represented by someone junior in the meeting and therefore less likely to be heard?

Before you begin to engage in the task at hand, engage in a quick conversation about who is present. Draw a MindTime Map on a piece of paper and plot a dot on the map for each person, representing their thinking style.

The first few times you do this you might feel very awkward; we are not used to talking about the dynamics in the group, it's like pointing out that there's an elephant in the room. If you find that there is something amiss in the make-up of the group, you're going to have to do something about it. And that can be a drag. But I think that it is more of a drag to waste life in trying to achieve goals that are all but impossible given the ingredients at hand. Try baking a cake without using any liquids.

7

TURNING THE WHEEL OF INNOVATION

We now turn to the Wheel of Innovation. It will show you how to combine your group's talents and begin the process of co-creation.

Innovation requires more than just creativity, it requires all perspectives to become aligned and collaborate effectively.

The Wheel provides a structure that tells you when it's time to brainstorm, when it's time to test out new ideas, and when it's time to put them into action.

An organization operates most effectively when it is guided by the Wheel of Innovation.

The Wheel always begins with Future thinking.

Future thinking serves the same purpose for a group as it does for an individual: its energy shakes up people's thinking and opens up new possibilities, it grasps the big picture, anticipates change, sees novel approaches, and generates enthusiasm by describing the complex future in simple terms and metaphors.

When a group engages in Future thinking, it is fully energized. Sparks fly. Creative individuals inspire and support each other. They bounce new ideas off each other, make new connections, and come up with unexpected insights. This all happens as if by magic. This is the essence of the brainstorming process.

For this to occur there must be no judgment.

For this to occur there must be no judgment. The silliest and

73

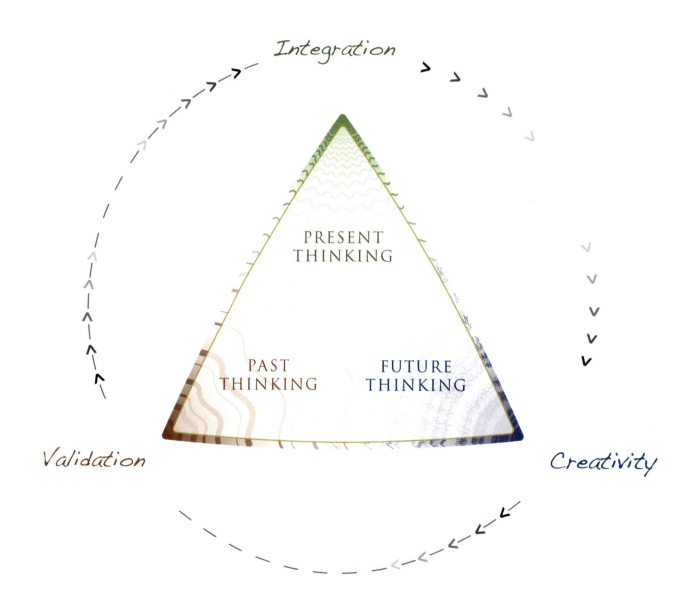

Integration

PRESENT
THINKING

PAST
THINKING

FUTURE
THINKING

Validation

Creativity

most outrageous ideas must be encouraged as they feed off each other energetically, stimulating new ways of thinking about things. Professor Edward De Bono calls this Lateral Thinking, and most of us know it as "thinking out of the box."

The Past thinkers must be patient and resist the temptation to demand that these creative ideas meet a certain litmus test.

This lack of structure and suspension of judgment allows Future thinking to do what it does best.

When Future thinking is in control (seemingly out-of-control), the energy of the group is light-hearted and full of banter, the conversation non-linear and full of free association.

The tempo can be rapid and frenetic as these creative minds engage each other. This can make Present and Past thinkers a little uncomfortable, but it's the price one pays for creativity.

In the Past-thinking phase, the group begins to shift its energy. They weigh the evidence and *validate* the creative ideas that have come out of the brainstorming phase.

There's a distinct shift in tempo as the group enters a reflective mode.

There's a distinct shift in tempo as the group enters a reflective mode. This phase can take a good deal more time because people need to collect information, deliberate, and test alternative scenarios. Much of this work can be done independently, but at some point the group starts to debate the pros and cons of each approach, review competing strategies, and decide which new idea has the best chance of succeeding.

The speed of competition drives businesses to move as quickly as they can from idea to market penetration in their quest for an innovative lead.

The Present-thinking phase begins only when you have a valid option. Now the group gears up for action, assigning probabilities, establishing benchmarks, defining procedures, and deciding how to measure outcomes. This phase represents an *integration* of all that has come before: creativity and validation at last come together in practical execution. The tempo changes yet again, and this time we get the steady pulse of daily work—the heart of any enterprise.

Key tasks of the phases of collaboration

Why is it that we insist on flowing our energies from Future to Present and only after there has been failure, to Past?

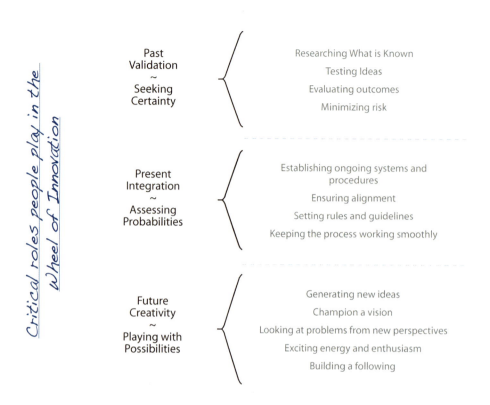

Critical roles people play in the Wheel of Innovation

Past Validation ~ Seeking Certainty
- Researching What is Known
- Testing Ideas
- Evaluating outcomes
- Minimizing risk

Present Integration ~ Assessing Probabilities
- Establishing ongoing systems and procedures
- Ensuring alignment
- Setting rules and guidelines
- Keeping the process working smoothly

Future Creativity ~ Playing with Possibilities
- Generating new ideas
- Champion a vision
- Looking at problems from new perspectives
- Exciting energy and enthusiasm
- Building a following

The answer is two-fold. First, the speed of competition drives businesses to move as quickly as they can from idea to market penetration in their quest for an innovative lead. That means that while Past thinkers might be shouting from the roof tops in disagreement, there is a powerful force that moves things from Future to Present- it's called opportunity cost and is driven by need for profit.

Second, people will tend to follow an intuitive linear mode of thinking, moving from Future to Present, when they communicate their vision.

Moving Collaboratively around the Innovation Cycle

Future thinkers like to keep moving their ideas forward. They love expounding their ideas and can go on brainstorming forever.

In a situation like this, Past thinkers, who are typically among the most quiet and introverted people, aren't likely to step in and assert themselves, not unless something is really wrong and threatening them. So how do you set the boundary for ending the free-form thinking and moving on?

The solution is simple: agree on a deadline at the very start: brainstorming will end when the meeting is over at 3 o'clock, or in six weeks, and so on.

The deadline will, of course, be arbitrary, but remember, Future thinkers will keep on tossing out new ideas until the end of time. You have to put a limit on a process that's potentially infinite.

The good news is that a deadline can also stimulate Future thinking to a higher level of creativity. Future thinkers are known for putting things off and being terrifically creative at the very last moment— routinely pulling the rabbit out of the hat.

But you also have to be concerned about how the fragile seeds created by the Future folks are handed off to their colleagues. This is often a delicate moment and you have to be careful not to bruise the egos of the Future thinkers and to avoid personality conflicts.

Past thinkers now have the permission to control the conversation, and they're likely to say, "Hell no, that's not a good idea," or "Man, this sure won't work." If this is how the ideas of Future thinkers are met they they will start to dig in their heels and you have a battle of wills.

The key to a successful handoff is this: You need to tell Past thinkers that they are being entrusted with fragile and valuable seeds and help them find a new vocabulary.

The key to a successful handoff is this: You need to tell Past thinkers that they are being entrusted with fragile and valuable seeds and help them find a new and more constructive vocabulary.

They must replace negative words like *no, won't,* and *can't* with words of support and gratitude, saying to the Future Thinkers, "Thank you for these exciting possibilities! Let's find out which are the strongest and the best, so we can add more understanding and insight to them."

Future thinkers need to feel honored and know that others care enough about their ideas to put them through an elaborate evaluation process, often a huge investment of other people's time.

Nay-saying is then transformed into celebration and encouragement.

The Future thinkers know that not all their ideas will survive, but they are happy to have kicked off the next phase of the innovation cycle.

The next challenge is negotiating the transition from validation to action/integration. This phase, too, can go sour if you don't decide on a hand-over date. Analysis paralyses can set in and all forward progress arrested.

Past thinkers are eager to continue exploring, collecting more and more information, to reach a higher level of certainty. There's rarely a point at which the validation process reaches a natural conclusion. Therefore, the leader has to decide when enough is enough.

Tending to the Wheel of Collaboration—and making sure all thinking styles are honored—is the leader's job.

Unlike brainstorming, validation shouldn't be tied to and bound by an arbitrary deadline. You can't know up front how long due diligence is going to take. So what the group must do is come up with a definition of what constitutes acceptable risk: at what point will you know enough to move forward with a reasonable expectation of success?

To gauge whether you've reached an acceptable level of risk, ask yourself, "To what degree have my people bought in to this project?" At some point, enough of them will back the idea, and enough evidence will have stacked up behind it, that everyone can feel comfortable moving forward.

During this transition, the Past thinkers can do the Present thinkers a great favor if they sift through all the information they've collected, set aside what's irrelevant, and give them a good summary of the relevant details.

Present thinkers want only the most pertinent facts and salient information, what's necessary for making plans, setting up timeframes, and getting things done. They want conclusions, not the logical steps that lead to them; they want to see trends and patterns, not the individual data points that make them up.

Valuing the contribution each person brings to the table...

If the Future thinkers and Past thinkers have done their jobs well, the Present thinkers will be fully energized and eager to proceed—doing what boosts *their* self-esteem: producing, executing, and bringing the process to completion.

Mastering the Many Levels of Innovation

A group is often involved in more than one collaborative cycle at a time. Some of these may run their course during a half-hour committee meeting, while others play out over weeks, months, or even years.

Tending to the Wheel of Innovation—and making sure all thinking styles are honored—is the leader's job.

You need to remind the group where they are in the innovation cycle, oversee the transition from one phase to another, remind people to be conscious of their language and show respect for thinking styles that are often wildly different from their own.

You also need to model the basic premise of this work, valuing the contribution each person brings to the table, and showing them how they can work together to fulfill their larger mission.

The more committed you are to this process, the more rapidly your group will achieve its goals.

In short, an understanding of thinking styles is what makes you as a leader—and your entire organization—begin to soar.

Exercise:
Reading People

"Everyone has value to bring." We call this the Golden Thought.

How satisfying it is to read a person and understand and empathize with their world view, and perhaps have them do the same for you.

Here is the first step. Practice asking yourself this question whenever you meet a person: What is this person's value? What contribution are they making to the world with their thinking? We coined the Golden Thought as a thought that we could all hold in our minds when working with others.

This simple thought begins the process of paying attention to the other person. As you do, you will begin to notice this person's thinking at work. You'll begin to recognize their thinking style and needs.

I like to practice this when listening to people being interviewed or making a speech on the radio. It's amazing how much you can learn about a person when you simply listen and use the MindTime framework to reference what you are hearing. Practice this and you will actually become quite good at reading people; they will become less of a mystery to you.

8

MindTime and Its Many Uses

" Wherever you go, there you are."

This quote is most apt for the beginning of this chapter; people's thinking is at work whether they're diligently doing their jobs, browsing the bookshelves of their neighborhood bookstore, or tweeting a fleeting thought. It's like a mental finger print and it shows up on everything their attention touches on. Peoples' thinking dictates their needs, preferences, values and the choices they make. It colors their experience of life and how they engage with their world. It's also an incredibly telling and predictable aspect of their make-up. It is highly observable everywhere, when you know what your looking for.

My work with people using MindTime has been predominantly in an organizational development setting. Ironically my very first consulting job using MindTime was helping a client to write a better classified advertisement to attract a rainmaker to an accounting company. It worked! Today, that first exercise in MindTime driven messaging seems almost a prediction of things to come. As we embark on bringing MindTime to the world as a way of helping people understand people, embedded as it can be in our social fabric, we see uses only limited by our human imaginations.

On the pages following, I've provided just a handful of the MindTime applications that we have explored. We welcome your thoughts and ideas.

1. Leadership. There's a new kind of knowledge in our world—meta-knowledge—this is the understanding of how knowledge behaves as it moves around organizations and how each thinking perspective adds value to it. Leaders of every kind need to understand this meta-knowledge, it reveals important insight about the culture of an organization and how to message, lead, manage change, foster collaboration, and understand the fundamental driving forces that shape and define all people's thinking. Organizations are thinking systems at work.

2. Collaboration. MindTime helps you to build more effective and responsive teams. It shows you how to get the "right mix" of thinking styles for the job. Even more, MindTime provides a simple language for everyone to understand individual contribution and identify how best to collaborate.

3. Human Performance. MindTime shows what gets people excited about their jobs. It reveals the deep connections between the roles people play and their thinking styles. This encourages them to perform at higher levels. It can also help you design more effective compensation and reward systems.

4. The Cycle of Innovation. Innovation should be the prevailing mantra in every organization. CEOs and managers need to harness what McKinsey calls, "The irrational forces of change." MindTime gives you a map of the Innovation Cycle and shows which thinking style should lead each phase of the innovation process. MindTime also helps you understand and anticipate the pace you can expect adoption of new ideas to happen at in different areas of the organization. Unrealistic expectations in this regard only cause unnecessary stress and resistance.

5. Employee wellness and job satisfaction. The cost of healthcare has made employee wellness a hot topic. It is one of the only ways of reducing healthcare costs. The relationship between people and their jobs, the environment they work in, their sense of self-determination, predictability of their work day, relationship with co-workers and their immediate supervisors, and many other factors, are behind employee stress levels, and of course both sick days and healthcare costs. MindTime has successfully been used to survey organizations to measure job satisfaction and even predict likely areas of stress for each thinking style.

6. Education. Good training is critical to any organization's success. However, people with different thinking styles require different stimuli, curricula and different learning environments. This seems obvious. Yet for years most corporate training has been one-size-fits-all. The Web is ideally suited to customizing the learning experience to individuals' learning style. Designing online training using MindTime principles promises to change the learning experience and individuals' success rate.

7. Sales. Every truly great sales person knows that making a deal is a complex dance. Understanding a prospect's thinking style can help you build instant rapport, cultivate trust, and increase the chances of closing the deal.

8. Conflict Resolution. MindTime Maps, with their powerful survey tools, have been used to understand ongoing conflicts in organizations. In short, MindTime provides a way to "unpack" employee disagreements by revealing the connection between people's points of view and their thinking style. Resolving conflict is really about creating understanding, allowing people to feel heard, and honoring different points of view.

9. Time Awareness. MindTime helps people organize their work days to achieve maximum productivity. But, there is much more to it than that. One of the insights you will gain about your organization is each individual's and each department's sense of time. Asking Past thinkers to certify data as quickly as Future thinkers come up with ideas is simply not rational. That does not mean one should ignore Past thinking to speed things up (a frequent and often tragic mistake made by managers and leaders). Understanding the time frames of the different thinking styles can help you plan for innovation in rational and effective ways.

10. Client engagement. MindTime explains how to understand a client's needs and ensure that people with the "right" thinking style are selected to work most closely with a client. It can show you how to create pitch teams that have a far higher likelihood of success with new customers or clients. In fact, the whole world of Customer Relationship Management benefits from MindTime insights. Including messaging, frequency, preferences, communication style and informational needs. All are more informed by this simple idea.

11. Global Business. In today's global organizations it is common for people to work with colleagues they've never actually met face-to-face. This lack of physical presence robs people of the ability to "read" someone in that way that is only really possible in person. It robs co-workers of an essential sense about each other. MindTime Maps can help you combat this deficiency by revealing individuals' thinking styles and informing each person of what to expect and teach people how to better understand their colleagues and co-workers.

12. Advertising and Marketing. MindTime is an extraordinary tool for advertisers and marketers as well. It helps them understand their various audiences and even predict responses to different messages. All human behavioral data can be better understood using the MindTime Framework revolutionizing your ability to target market, message, and reach out to a specific consumer group.

13. Web Analytics. By integrating MindTime with Web analytics applications, we are able to identify the unique patterns of behavior among Web users. This is valuable information you can share with potential advertisers. It is also a smart way to think about content, design and navigation schemas. The value of being able to track, segment and understand Web audiences in this way is considerable because it provides a means to increase traffic retention. In fact, it may be that MindTime provides the first set of psychological design principles for Web architects and designers.

14. Audience Segmentation (and persona building). Building sound relationships requires a deeper understanding of people. It also requires engaging with them in such a way as to meet their unstated needs and preferences across many touch points. By revealing the invisible forces of thinking at work, MindTime allows marketers to identify and cater to the fundamental differences in people—and speak directly to different segments of their audience.

15. Brand Behaviors. Brand Behaviors are how an organization treats its customers and keeps its promises. They are also fundamental to building brand value and equity. They infuse the customer's mind with the expereince of the brand. MindTime not only reveals the audiences thinking style, but also your organization's consumer touch points in the form of your people. In call centers, retail floors, front desks and aircarft cabins, it is people who are building (or destroying) your brand. Understanding the relationship between your employees thinking style and their brand behaviors is essential to building trust and confidence in your product or service.

There are resources on our Web site at www.mindtime.com, or visit mindtimemaps.com to try our mapping tools; or email us: contact@mindtime.com. We hope that you will write about and share your discoveries and applications for MindTime with others; use the tag - MindTime - on the Web.

The Worlds of **mindtime** Innovation

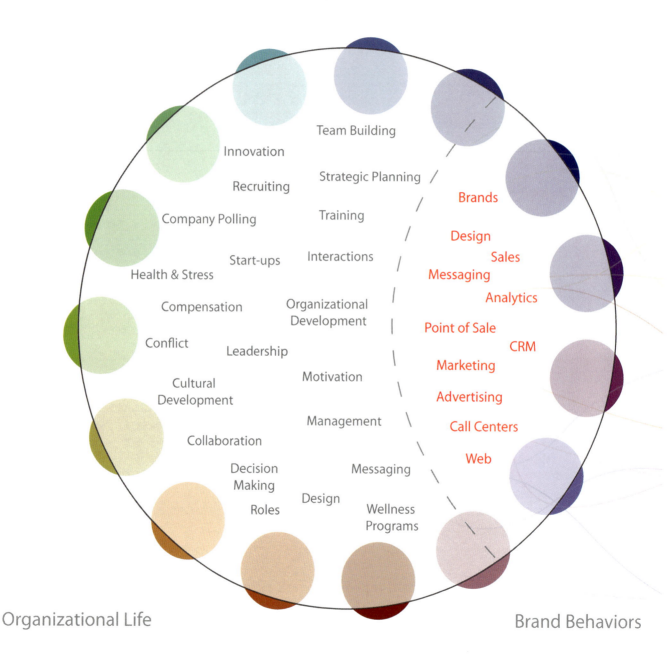

Team Building

Innovation

Recruiting

Strategic Planning

Company Polling

Training

Start-ups

Interactions

Health & Stress

Compensation

Organizational
Development

Conflict

Leadership

Cultural
Development

Motivation

Collaboration

Management

Decision
Making

Messaging

Roles

Design

Wellness
Programs

Brands

Design

Sales

Messaging

Analytics

Point of Sale

CRM

Marketing

Advertising

Call Centers

Web

Organizational Life

Brand Behaviors

MindTime is a universal organizing principle. It reveals people's thinking at work in many aspects of organizational life, it informs how organizations should interface with their markets, and it humanizes a myriad of products and services.

Peace

Industrial Design

Statistics

Opinion Research

Political Campaigns

Information Architecture

Infographics

Interface

Web Analytics   Education   Consumer Intelligence

Mobile Apps

Healthcare

Web Design   Design Principles

Games

Diplomacy

Human Potential

Economics   Product Design   Guest Services

IM / SMS   Dating & Relationships

Blogs

Standardized Testing   Governance

Mind Research

Brand Behavior   Online

Global Solutions

Publishing   Mind Ergonomics

Community Build

Email   Psychology

Preference Engines

Office Workspace Design

Analytics   Financial Markets

Social Anthropology   Services

Market Applications

FREQUENTLY ASKED QUESTIONS ABOUT MINDTIME.

I disagree with my Time Style. Why?

There are many possible answers to this. First, did you answer the questions based on how you really are, or on how you think you want people to see you? The great thing about MindTime is that there's no better or worse, so if you think you nudged the results, go back and try again. You may also want to ask yourself why you nudged the results or why you don't agree with your Time Style. If you're recognizing traits you don't want to admit to, then you're in luck! This is exactly what we're here to show you--how you can change how you make decisions if the way you're doing it now limits your success or happiness.

I agree with 95 percent of my Time Style, but I think 5 percent is way off. Why?

The beauty of the MindTime model is that it is precise in its generalities. Since we're human, we cannot be pinpointed with 100 percent accuracy. This is why most people are bothered by those personality tests that pigeonhole you into one way of being. While you may follow most of the traits of your Time Style, there will be situations when you don't. We all use the future, present, and past perspectives when we manage life and it's impossible to gauge if there are specific situations where you might use a thinking perspective that you normally don't. Since we're so wonderfully complicated, there are times when we do something that appears to have no real reason. So someone who is a strong Future thinker might suddenly do something that you'd expect from someone with a strong past or present thinking style. In fact, some people find the real fascination with their Time Style not in what they usually do, but in these many little exceptions.

Does my Time Style ever change?

It can, in some ways. And you can also do something about changing your behavior, if you want. MindTime was designed to give you an easy way to think about how your behavior is a consequence of the decisions you make. These may be conscious decisions driven by a sub-conscious process, or they can be simply sub-conscious decisions. So if you know your Time Style as it stands today, it gives you some reference point about how you're seeing the world and how you work with it. If the results you are currently getting from how you do things are not what you want, then MindTime can show you how you can change the decision-making process you use to adopt one that will achieve the desired result. This is the function of self-aware discipline. However, it is unlikely that, without a concerted, long-term practice, you will fundamentally change the way you are wired to think.

Okay. So how can I change now?

Right. This is sounding like the "Lord, give me patience and give it to me NOW!" routine. We're not offering: "Do this now and you'll be changed forever." We're here to create conscious awareness. Changing the way you make decisions is not like changing the color of your hair. It takes time and mindfulness. You need to understand what you're doing and see how people who use other thinking styles do things and then compare, contrast, and experiment.

Is this like a Myers Briggs?

No. The Myers Briggs is what we call a personality test: it measures a very small number of personality traits and specifically how you score relative to a population group (the famous bell curve). MindTime does not measure you against other people, but shows where you stand within a natural phenomenological structure, in our case, time. It is not a comparative, human-to-human, type of exercise.

How did I come to have this Time Style?

Ah, the perennial question of nature versus nurture. One of our goals at the MindTime Project is to work on answering that question satisfactorily. Does that sound like a cop-out? In a way, it is. We honestly can't say, although since we note that people, after becoming aware of their Time Style, are able to make at least some changes, this goes a long way towards suggesting nurture plays a big role. But there is also a lot to be said for people being born with a natural proclivity (perhaps genetic) towards one Time Style over another. We hope that one day we will be able to answer this question more fully.

Does my Time Style limit me in any way?

Only you can decide that. MindTime is not about whom or what is best, just about which Time Style is better conditioned for specific tasks and situations. For example, someone who uses Past thinking works better with lots of detailed information than a person using Future thinking, who's comfortable making decisions with less information (by the seat of their pants, to be more specific). If you ask a Past thinker to make a snap decision without giving them the time and resources to investigate the pros and cons, they're going to be less prepared than the Future thinker (and probably a great deal more stressed at the prospect). Neither thinking style is wrong, but the Past thinker may feel limited in that specific situation.

ACKNOWLEDGMENTS

True to its topic, this book has been a wonderfully collaborative effort. Eric Engles, Ph.D., Louie Simon, Ph.D., Vince Fortunato, Ph.D., Valerie Andrews, and Shawn Phillips each posed intriguing questions and contributed to the development of this book.

Shawn Phillips, Vince Fortunato and Irwin Sentilles—my business partners and friends—have become an integral part of this project over the past five years.

The rest of my team have been nothing short of inspirational. Anne Doremus helped pull together our case histories and many years of notes, which made the writing process a great deal easier. Sylvie Pellet's work on my previous collaborative book written with Miller Stevens, *Power Tools: A User's Manual for the Mind*--set high standards for this handbook.

Psychologist, colleague, and early MindTime enthusiast Veda Ball has been a valuable sounding board since the mid-90s. Professor Dan Ariely, formerly of the Massachusetts Institute of Technology, and author of *Predictably Irrational,* was my colleague in the development of the Time Style Profile in 1998. He also performed the validation studies on it and has provided encouragement ever since.

Former California State Senator and Judge Lawrence Stirling insisted that I write this handbook and provided unequivocal support and encouragement for many years of exploration and research.

Glen, Darren, Jim, Alan, Nate, Larry, Ann, Muffy, Morrigan, and

Cheri provided a special class of help, financial help. Over the years, their generosity has enabled us to develop and bring MindTime to a larger audience.

I'm also grateful to Kathy Kolbe. Her approach to understanding people influenced my early thoughts and helped lead me to my present understanding of the world in which we think.

I'd like to give special thanks to John A. Casey P.E. I rarely meet people who commit to getting something done and then do it with such integrity, generosity, and support. In some ways it is thanks to John's enthusiastic support and excellent suggestions made after multiple readings of an earlier manuscript, that this book exists today.

While there have been many people involved in the development of MindTime over the years, I am solely responsible for the contents of this book.

We've used a few generic examples in this book, and most of the time, we've relied on case histories, changing the names of the main players to protect our clients' privacy.

ABOUT THE AUTHOR

John Furey founded the MindTime Project in 1997 to explore his deep interest in human thinking more formally. He worked with scientists, thought leaders, psychologists, and management experts to develop MindTime, a unique and scientifically validated theory of individual differences. He has authored two books, co-authored several scientific papers, and spoken to business and academic audiences in the United States, Europe, and Australia. He has consulted with The Nature Conservancy, the Royal Bank of Canada, Merrill Lynch, Hewlett Packard, and many other organizations. He was raised in Switzerland and educated in England. He lived in Africa for a number of years before moving to the United States and becoming a pioneer in the field of management consulting.

SPACE FOR YOUR OBSERVATIONS ABOUT MINDTIME

Made in the USA
San Bernardino, CA
20 August 2013